THE ART OF IT LEADERSHIP

Essential Skills for an IT Career

MICHAEL SCHEUERMAN
MANOJ GARG

Virtual Information Executives, LLC

Portland, Oregon

The Art of IT Leadership

Published by:

Virtual Information Executives, LLC

12639 NW Waker Drive, Portland, OR 97229

www.viellc.com/resources/the-art-of-it-leadership

information@viellc.com

ISBN (Print): 978-1-66784-070-3

ISBN (eBook): 978-1-66784-071-0

Also published simultaneously in eBook format

For bulk ordering copies of this book, please contact VIE at information@viellc.com

Cover design by: BookBaby

Book design by: BookBaby

Printed in the United States of America

Table of Contents

Acknowledgements

This book is dedicated to our spouses, Judy (Mike) and Jackie (Manoj) who have enabled our careers by being pillars of support. We also wish to thank Afton Nelson; without her help and dedication, this book would not have seen the light of day. We would also like to thank our clients who, over the years, have placed their faith in us and allowed us to look deeply into their organizations and learn what we hope is conveyed in this book.

We also would like to thank all those who read and commented on the rough drafts of the book. Their input is greatly appreciated and contributed to making this book much better. Lastly, we would like to thank our consulting colleagues for sharing key insights and ideas about how IT should function within business.

Mike Scheuerman

Manoj Garg

April 2022

Introduction

The Art of IT Leadership is a business novel that educates senior IT leaders how to get an edge in running their IT departments through the strategic use of Information Technology and management processes. It gives readers the knowledge and tools to guide their company as it transitions from a mid-level to a high-level competitor in the marketplace. It takes the wondering out of the picture and shows IT leaders what key skills they need to develop and improve to become more effective leaders. Through its narrative, it simultaneously tells the tale of a Chief Information Officer as he makes a set of progressive transitions in his career.

Most IT leaders start their career in a technical role in IT. As their career progresses, they improve their technical skills (technical diagnosis, design, implementation, etc.) substantially. However, to be an effective IT leader, they also need strong customer facing skills including communication, empathy, and the ability to build trust with customers. To learn the needed skills requires patience, diligence, and practice. We wrote this book to help these leaders. Through the story of his career and life, we show how the central character – Gordon, encounters opportunities to learn these skills and leverage them to become a truly effective leader.

Developing IT leaders wonder if they need to learn new skills and transform. Some of the question they are asking include:

- How can IT leader develop strong relationships with other executives and work closely with them on business and IT initiatives? How to speak the language of business?

- How to build and sustain an IT organization that is capable, effective, and efficient?

- How to understand or infer business strategy and how to build a robust, aligned IT strategic plan?

- How to use new technologies to increase automation in the business as well as create new product and services for end customers?

- How to manage IT projects successfully for optimal outcomes?

We answer all these questions and more in this book.

We coined the term - 'IT Value Pyramid' to succinctly capture the three key roles of the Information Technology department and function in any organization. Essentially, IT is an integrating function that serves to glue various information systems and diverse business processes together to form the value chain for customers. It may help to think in terms of the three key and distinct roles of IT and how any IT department can work to perform them well.

These are:

- IT-as-Dial Tone provider (Service Provider),
- IT-as-a-Lever (Partner) and

- IT-as-a-Driver (Leader).

We wrote this book as a business novel to explain the concepts behind the 'IT Value Pyramid' through an easy-to-follow interesting story about a true-to-life character.

For the reader who does not have the time to read the novel, they can skip to the Tools and Tips section at the end of the book for a quick education on how to manage IT for maximum business value.

Chapter 1
June, 1992

Gordon Rusbart followed the signs through a maze of halls into the bowels of the student center. In his four years at the University of Colorado, he'd never had occasion to explore this part of the building. Most of his comings and goings had been to the bookstore two floors above, or to the C4C dining hall for a weekly taco salad and Coke. Navigating the windowless halls of basement level 2 felt like a rite of passage, and he suspected he wasn't alone in that feeling, especially when he saw the line snaking out of B2-104, the location of cap and gown pick up.

Gordon was renting, not buying. Growing up on a farm in the Nebraska panhandle had taught him resilience and common sense, and had given him a belief that a much-needed eleventh commandment should read: *Thou shalt be thrifty*. No need to spend money to purchase something he'd wear just once. He smiled at the young woman who held the black robes to his shoulders, did a quick check for length, and proclaimed it perfect.

"You can pick your cap up over there." She gestured to a series of clear tubs on a table filled with plastic-wrapped mortar boards. "Then just check out at the register and you're good to go. Oh, and congratulations on your graduation." She winked and Gordon resisted the urge to ask for her number. After this week, he'd be back in Nebraska, working for the family farm and hopefully making some positive changes. He'd had several ideas about using computers to automate some of the farm tasks. The real challenge would be getting his dad to give up his old paper ledgers and try something new. It would be a hurdle, but no doubt one that Gordon could clear.

Working for the farm wasn't a passion for Gordon, but plans to go to medical school pretty much deteriorated when he considered the cost, combined with his GPA. He'd done well in school, but anatomy and organic chemistry had taken a back seat once he started working in the computer lab. He'd enjoyed his job at the help desk so much that he often stayed late when he should have been back at his apartment, studying for quizzes.

With his gown slung over his arm and his cap tucked under, Gordon stepped on the elevator and pressed the button for his floor. His parents and brother were arriving later tonight, and he probably should make his bed before his mom showed up and started inspecting things. The elevator doors opened and Gordon exited toward the bookstore, weaving through an end of semester art show set up in the student lounge. He considered picking up a sandwich in the Grab-n-Go.

"Hello, Gordon."

Startled from his train of thought, Gordon pulled up short to see Ann, the computer lab manager, standing in front of a still life of a bowl of fruit. This was good luck. Ann was on his short list of people to say goodbye to. She'd not only been his manager, she'd also acted as mentor, challenging him with new opportunities to learn and advance in his job.

"Looks like you're all ready for graduation," she said, nodding to the yards of fabric draped over his arm.

"Yeah, just wrapping up a few loose ends before my family arrives."

"That's wonderful. Listen," Ann said, pivoting the conversation without skipping a beat. She was organized, thorough, and hated wasting time, a work ethic that seeped neatly into her personal life as well. "I know you talked about going back to Nebraska after graduation. That still the plan?"

"Yep. My dad's already got a list of jobs he wants me to tackle." The farm was good, solid work. Consistent. And he knew what he was doing on the farm. He'd grown up working it. There would be no surprises. Nice and steady. Plus, his family was there. Grandparents, cousins, aunts and uncles. He thought fondly of the big family dinners and holiday get togethers he'd be a part of.

"Well, if there's any wiggle room, I have a great opportunity I think you'd be perfect for."

He'd just put new tires on his car for the drive home and his dad said he was looking forward to his help for the corn harvest in two weeks. Plans had been made.

"The university needs to update their payroll system to comply with new requirements from the Social Security Administration. It's a huge coding project and would be a salaried, full-time job. It could be the start of a career. I'll be managing the project and can't think of anyone better to work with than you."

Almost reluctantly, Gordon noticed an internal surge of interest. He'd enjoyed writing code at the lab and Ann was so detailed with her instructions, it made his job straightforward. And more than that, satisfying. Nothing was better than putting in a list of commands and watching the computer bend to your will. It was probably the reason he'd gotten a B minus in organic chemistry and a C in anatomy, the rules weren't quite as precise.

But he'd already committed to his dad. He was expecting him to come home. On top of that, his lease was up on his apartment at the end of the week. Half of his stuff was already boxed up, ready to go.

"I think I better stick with my plans," he told Ann. "Wheels are already in motion. And who knows. Maybe I can convince my dad to let me write a payroll system for him." The farm was in desperate need of some automation and Gordon planned to make those changes. Just thinking about how much work he could save his dad, and how much he could help grow profits … he was pretty excited about it, actually.

Ann nodded but looked a little disappointed. "I hope you find a way to work with computers on the farm, because you've got talent. It would be a shame to waste it." A smile tugged at the corner of her mouth, and he knew her little guilt trip was meant with love. "If you change your mind, though, you know where to find me." She nodded again and strode off without another word. Gordon was glad for her lack of sentimentality. He'd spent four years working with her, and he would miss her. But avoiding an emotional display was always a bonus, as far as he was concerned.

* * *

The waiter set a large sausage pizza in the middle of the table. The Brick Oven was, by far, not the fanciest restaurant in town, but it was nicer than Gordon's college budget allowed, so it made a fine spot for a graduation dinner. Gordon's brother Brett pulled a slice onto his plate, letting the long string of cheese hang before hooking it with his finger and sticking it in his mouth.

"Brett," Mom chastised. "This isn't a horse stable. Remember your manners." Brett rolled his eyes. He was three years older than Gordon and hadn't, according to him, *wasted* time at college but instead gone right to work on the farm. He was a foreman now, and had even bought a little house of his own a few miles from the farm. An actual *horse stable* came with the property, and Brett planned to board for a little extra income.

"Well, son." Gordon's dad looked a little nostalgic. He'd attended CU, too. This was where he'd met Gordon's mom. But he'd left after two years to go back and work on the farm when many young men were headed off to Vietnam and farm workers were scarce, and he'd never come back to finish his degree. "This is a big accomplishment." Next to him Brett huffed but quickly covered it up with a cough. Mom passed him her water and a stern look. "We're real proud of you."

"Thanks, Dad." Gordon would have told him he was grateful for his support. His dad had put up with lots of snide comments from friends who thought a university education was a waste of time when a perfectly good job was waiting for his son on the farm. He would have told him that he appreciated his sacrifice—of having one less set of hands to help out. He even would have told him he loved him. But all of that would have embarrassed both of them and made Brett choke for real, so he left it at *Thanks*.

"Your mom and I wanted to get you a little something ..." Dad started.

Gordon protested. "Aww, you didn't have to do anything."

"No, no," Dad said, and Mom reached across the table and gave Gordon's hand a squeeze. "You worked hard. None of my friends' kids paid for their own tuition and housing costs like you did. This is a big deal."

"Most didn't bother with college," Brett said under his breath.

Dad hefted an oblong, wrapped box onto the table, causing it to wobble under the box's weight. Gordon's mom steadied her water glass.

Gordon hadn't expected anything and was touched by the gesture.

"Go ahead," Mom said. "Open it."

He caught the paper under the seam and tore it off. What had he expected? A briefcase? Luggage? A pair of cufflinks? He was going to work on a farm, for crying out loud. He wouldn't need any of that. But the actual gift still caught him off guard. The red steel case was the first thing he saw. Two chrome clasps and a handle on top finished it off. It was a toolbox. A really good one, if he remembered his brands correctly.

"Wow." It was all he could think to say. It was the kind of thing that would last his whole life, as long as he didn't let it fall out of his pickup on the freeway.

"Go ahead. Open it." His dad looked on with pride as Gordon undid the latches. The box split down the middle and two tiered shelves accordioned out on either side, each shelf filled with tools. There was a ratchet set, several sizes of screwdrivers, a family of wrenches, and a hefty claw hammer with a shock-resistant grip on a steel handle.

The gift was as generous as it was practical. These were quality tools that would be useful whether he lived in an apartment in the city or at home on the farm. But he wouldn't be in an apartment in the city. He'd be on the farm.

"I know it's not a new car or a trip to Europe," his dad said.

"That's what the article in *Reader's Digest* said were good graduation gifts," his mom added.

"I would have refused a trip to Europe anyway," Gordon said. "I would never let you spend that much money on me."

"That's what I said." His dad threw out his hands before bringing them down on the table, like he'd just won a bet. "Besides, you can drive the Ford. It's still under a hundred thousand on the odometer. That will handle the dirt roads through the fields just fine."

"Practically brand new." Gordon smiled and thanked his parents again for the tools while Brett stuffed another slice of pizza into his mouth in three bites. Gordon shut the box, carefully folding the sides back together. He set the box on the floor at his feet, the slice of pizza he'd just eaten feeling like a brick in his stomach. Was this his life now? A toolbox in the back of an old pickup truck? A lifetime of physical labor? He had nothing against hard work—physical work. But he looked at his dad, a man not yet out of his forties, who already looked to be sixty. His skin tanned like leather and was just as thick with callouses.

There was nothing wrong with an honest days' work. Heck, he loved the feeling of working to exhaustion and coming home to a hot shower and a cold beer. That was satisfying. But forever? The same thing, day in, day out, season after season, year after year? He wasn't sure that would sustain him. Because what also felt satisfying was helping people solve computer problems. Writing programs. Making systems work more efficiently. Automating things.

Thank goodness he would do those kinds of things back home. It would be the best of both worlds. He'd be able to work the farm while also making the farm work better. That's the thing that excited him, and right now, it was the thought that calmed him as he grabbed another piece of pizza.

After dinner, Gordon dropped his family off at the Sleep Inn right off the freeway and headed back to his apartment. His mom had offered to take his graduation gown back to the hotel to iron it, but he'd refused, telling her he'd take care of it. He was pretty sure hanging it in the bathroom while he showered tomorrow would do the trick.

He thought about Ann and her job offer, but not because he was considering it. He wanted to make sure that whatever he ended up doing on the farm, he stirred up the same excitement and passion as that job offer had. The idea of creating a payroll program from scratch seemed thrilling. But it wasn't anything he couldn't do back on the farm, right?

He tossed and turned all night, dreaming of red steel toolboxes that turned into computers, and computers that turned into toolboxes. He sat through the commencement ceremony the next day, listening to speeches about persistence and success while looking for his family in the crowded stands. He posed for pictures under a tree in the quad while trying to memorize every last detail about this place.

Later, his dad and Brett watched a baseball game on his roommate's TV while his mom helped him pack his kitchen.

"You sure you don't want Brett to stay and drive back with you?" Mom used a dishtowel to wrap a dinner plate and set it in the box while Gordon tried to remember the last time he'd washed the towel.

"It's just three hours. I'll be fine to drive by myself. Besides, Brett's got to get back to help Dad." Honestly, it was a miracle they'd been able to take time off in the middle of the season. If they left in an hour, as planned, their whole trip would have lasted just over twenty-four hours.

"Okay, fine. Just make sure you bring something to snack on in case you get tired. Carrot sticks are good." His mom leaned around the corner to peek into the front room, then turned back to Gordon. "Just so you know, Dad is real glad you're coming back. I know you've been hoping to do some of your computer stuff to help out the farm, and son, I'm sure it would be a big help, but your dad is stubborn, and he likes doing things his way."

"I know, Mom. I grew up with him." Gordon put a handful of flatware into the box his mom was packing.

"What I'm saying is," she repositioned the silverware around the edges of the box and set another towel-wrapped plate on top of the stack. "He's probably not going to want to make any changes right away. You know, computer changes."

"That's fine. I don't expect him to buy computers next week. I can talk to him about my ideas. They usually have good sales around Thanksgiving. Maybe we can look at getting a couple then." Waiting until November or December to start writing programs for the farm would be difficult, but as long as it happened sooner rather than later, Gordon figured he'd be fine.

His mom stopped packing for a second and turned to face him. "Honey, I don't know. Just don't expect anything to change too soon."

"November's not soon," Gordon said.

His mom scrunched her face and made a noncommittal squeak as she slowly nodded her head.

"So, what? Next year? Summer?"

"Oh, gosh no. You know how busy things get in the summer." She picked up a plastic cup Gordon had gotten for free from the local minimart and set it in the box.

"Things wouldn't be as busy if I could set up some payroll and purchasing programs over the winter. That would be the perfect time to do it. Once I show Dad how much time he can save … it will make his life so much easier." Gordon took the plastic cup out of the box and tossed it into recycling. He'd graduated from school and also from plastic minimart cups.

"Honey." His mom let the word hang, and Dad and Brett let out a cheer in the front room at some exciting play in the game.

What was she saying? Would he never get to implement his ideas? Would he have to wait until his dad retired? That could be fifteen years. Maybe more. Gordon scrubbed his hands down his face. Knowing everything he knew about how helpful computers could be for the farm, it would be torture to have to work, day in and day out, doing things that would be easier, faster, and more efficient if they were automated. The thought made his heart ache.

He kept packing, though, right up until his family left an hour later. Then, for the last time, he went to meet his college friends at their favorite bar.

* * *

Gordon squinted against the sunlight that shot between the blinds like a laser beam. His head felt like it was splitting right down the middle and he held it between his hands as if this, alone, would keep it together. He hadn't planned on getting drunk, but finals had been hell, it had been a long week, and he deserved it.

At the bar last night, he'd listened while Gretchen talked about her job at a Big Five accounting firm in San Francisco. She beamed as she talked about her apartment in the city and how she was going to explore a different spot in the Bay Area every weekend. Even Gordon knew she'd probably be working weekends for at least the first year, but somehow, he still felt a twinge of jealousy.

Chapter 1

Erik was taking his degree in land management and working as a forest ranger at Yellowstone, the lucky bastard. Calvin had a job lined up at a small advertising firm in Salt Lake City, but to hear him talk about it, you'd think he'd be on Madison Avenue.

It was well after midnight when they left the bar and everyone hugged and clapped each other on the backs, promising to keep in touch.

"Good luck on the farm," Gretchen had said.

"You're a better man than me," Erik added. At the time, Gordon wasn't sure what he'd meant.

But now, here he was, at the intersection of before and after. All that was left to do was ball up his blanket and pillow, toss them in his car, and head north on Highway 25. Before he could head out of town, though, he had one last stop to make.

The rented graduation gown sat, wadded up, in a plastic bag. No need to keep it tidy now. It would go through the steam wash, get pressed and hung and ready for the next graduate. He turned in his keys to the landlord, looped his tassel over his rearview mirror, and drove to the C4C building. This time he knew right where to go. Elevators, two floors down, right, right, and then a left to B2-104.

The same young woman he'd seen a few days earlier sat on a stool behind the counter, reading a paperback. She looked up when he walked in. "Hi. How'd it go?"

Was she asking about graduation? How else would it go? "Great," he said. "So inspiring." Gordon nodded a little too enthusiastically.

She looked at him through narrowed eyes, a suspicious smile creeping onto her face. "Is that sarcasm I'm detecting?" She yanked the gown out of the bag and held it up, inspecting it for damage.

It was definitely sarcasm. Gordon had no illusions he'd be *taking the world by storm*. He was too practical to *follow his passion* or *go confidently toward his dreams*. "Maybe a little," he said.

"Well, I'll just mark that you returned the robe in good condition, and you can be on your way. I don't want to keep you from reaching for any stars, now."

Gordon chuckled lightly as the young woman tapped on a shiny new keyboard.

"Dang it," she said. "This thing keeps crashing. Sorry. Sometimes it helps to turn it off and on again." She reached down to the CPU and pressed the button a couple times. "This program was supposed to make my job easier, but so far, it's just a huge hassle." She tapped her fingers while she waited for the computer to come back on. "I mean how hard is it to write in a book that you returned your gown? Done and done, right?"

"How long have you had the new system? I'm Gordon, by the way."

"Tricia," the girl said. "We just got it this week."

"I know a few things about computers," Gordon said. "Let me have a look." He stepped behind the counter and Tricia moved to the side. "I used to work in the computer lab."

"Really? That's cool. So are you going to work with computers now that you've graduated?"

Gordon entered a few Excel commands and checked out the code, then entered a few more. It appeared someone had entered an incorrect formula on the spreadsheet. An easy fix. "I hope so," he said, but he knew then that he had to have more than hope. He couldn't commit to working on the farm and not be able to work with computers. He knew their potential and knew how to make them do what he wanted. Beyond that, he liked working with them.

No. He loved it. Dammit, *this* was his passion and he needed to go toward it, confidently.

The computer program popped up on the screen and Gordon searched for his name and checked his robe as *returned*.

"Wow, you're a natural. Maybe you should get a job here," Tricia said.

"Actually, I already have a job," Gordon said, and he hoped it was still true. "In fact, I have to go there now. I don't want to be late." He turned to leave. Maybe Ann was in her office now. All he knew was that he had to talk to her. Then he'd call his parents.

"Wait!" Tricia called. "You forgot your receipt."

"Thanks!" Gordon smiled as he grabbed it. He was halfway to the elevator when he noticed Tricia's number written on the back.

Chapter 2
October 1993

The scent of vanilla and chocolate assaulted Gordon as he looked at four identical cakes at the Boulder Bakery. "This is our buttercream icing," the cheerful woman said. Gordon thought her name was Joyce, but it could have been Jill. It was definitely something that started with J. "It's a classic and definitely a favorite for its taste. Now, if you want to go a little fancier, you could get the ganache."

"Oh," Tricia grabbed Gordon's arm. "That sounds nice."

"Very rich. Very decadent," Joyce-Jill said, flipping with gusto to a clean page in her spiral notebook to write something down. Most of the pages looked like they were holding on by just a few spirals.

"What do you think, Gordon?" Tricia and Joyce-Jill both looked at him expectantly.

"I agree," Gordon hoped this was the answer they were looking for. Cake shopping for his wedding was a singular kind of torture. Cake was cake. Why did it matter?

"You agree about what?" Tricia asked.

Oh no. A follow up question. "That the ganache is rich and decadent?" From the look on Tricia's face, he gathered he'd answered wrong. After a year of dating and three months of being engaged, he had a pretty good idea of what all her various looks meant.

"But which one do you think would be right for our wedding cake?" she asked through a tight smile.

"Both of them look delicious." He quickly realized this was also not the right answer, so he followed up with, "What's the price difference?"

Mistake.

Tricia and Joyce-Jill both launched into detailed speeches about why price wasn't the most important factor for a day as important as ones' wedding day. Maybe if Joyce-Jill were the one paying for it, she'd think differently. He and Tricia had a budget and if they overspent on the cake, they'd have to cut back in another area. Thankfully Joyce-Jill pushed a few cake samples their way and Gordon took the opportunity to shove one in his mouth rather than say all of this out loud.

The phone rang and Joyce-Jill jumped up to answer it, taking her notebook with her.

Cake shopping was not Gordon's idea of a good time. He'd told Tricia he would be fine with whatever wedding cake she wanted, as long as it was in the budget. Now, if he were writing a program for this bakery to upload customer orders with their inventory and purchasing requirements, that would be something he'd be interested in. Nothing as subjective as the best type of frosting, but hard, quantitative data that could be used to help run things more efficiently.

All at once the flavor and texture of the cake hit him. "Mmm. This is really good. Which one is this?"

Tricia smiled. "The ganache."

Gordon shook his head, feeling a little like a young bull being expertly corralled, and yet admiring her cleverness. "Then I vote for the ganache. This cake is amazing."

"Great choice." Joyce-Jill was back at the table. She pulled a pen out of her hairdo and glanced around, momentarily confused. "Now where did I put that notebook? Oh! There it is." She jumped up again to grab the notebook from where she'd left it by the phone and returned to the table, adding to her notes. Gordon had to hold back from asking her what her back-up plan was if she lost that book. He was pretty sure the book was the only place she wrote their names, phone number, and wedding date. She would have no way to contact them if something happened to it.

It was like Tricia could see the wheels turning in his head and knew exactly what he was thinking because she gave his knee a little squeeze, followed by a sweet and knowing look that said, *Let it go.*

Gordon couldn't help it. Once he started looking at business processes, all he could see was how things could be improved with technology. A year and half of working with Ann, writing programs to update the university's payroll system, had taught him that business efficiency was like an archeological dig. Once you peeled back one antiquated system, there was another begging for an update right below it.

Tricia squeezed his hand as they left the bakery, along with most of the contents of his wallet on a deposit with Joyce-Jill. "That wasn't so bad, was it?"

"Not once she brought out the cake." Gordon pulled her hand to his lips and kissed it.

"Do you have time for a quick trip to Foley's? You could help pick out our china pattern for the registry."

Gordon's pulse quickened and wondered if this is what the fight or flight response felt like. "Sorry," he said. "I've really got to get back to work." Thankfully, it was the truth.

"Have you talked to Ann about a raise yet?" Tricia had been bugging him about this for a few months now, but it never seemed like the right time to ask. He certainly deserved it. Ann, herself, had said he'd saved her bacon more than once. "If we're ever going to get a house this century, we really need to start saving."

"I know. I'll say something." Even with a raise, Gordon realized, saving enough for a house seemed like an unreachable dream. Once Tricia graduated in a few months, she'd quit her part-time, minimum wage job as a receptionist at the administration building and get a better job. But when they married, their expenses would go down, but if they were going to ever buy a home, he needed more than a little raise.

He watched Tricia drive off toward the mall as he slipped into his '82 Toyota Celica and made the familiar drive toward campus, letting his mind wander, just for fun, to just what kinds of improvements he could make at the bakery if given the chance. Recipes could be put into spreadsheets and synced up with inventory so Joyce-Jill would know exactly how much of each ingredient to purchase every week. She could keep track of best-selling products and use that data to make projections. She could even keep a database of her customers and their favorite desserts so she could send out targeted mailers. Mechanically, he turned from Colorado onto Regent then pulled into the parking lot across from the computer science building, his mind still buzzing. As soon as more people got email accounts, she could even set up a detailed email list that would save her even more on advertising.

His mind kept working as he locked his car, crossed the street, and felt the cool blast of the air conditioning as he entered the computer science building.

"There you are," Ann said as he threw his shoulder bag under the desk and tapped his keyboard to bring his computer to life. "Got the results from the beta testing on our updates. They loved your suggestion to change the home screen design. They're saying it's very user friendly."

"It just made sense to automate all the payroll deductions, and that new screen layout will make things much faster."

"Agreed. I can't believe you were able to get it all done. We're coming in right on schedule for this project."

It had taken more than a few late nights, but it felt good to be able to deliver a product.

"You still planning to take Friday off?" Ann pulled her rolling chair from across the room and took a seat next to his desk.

"Yeah. It's been a few months since I've been home for a visit. Tricia and my mom need to iron out wedding details. Dad wants me to help him set up a few spreadsheets on his new computer."

"Ah! He's finally coming around to technology?"

Gordon nodded. Ann had had a front row seat to the minor fallout that ensued when he'd told his dad he wasn't coming back to the farm after graduation. His dad had stewed for a few days, then called to tell Gordon he was still mad, but that he didn't blame him for taking the programming job. Gordon imagined his mother had had something to do with his softening. After six months on his university job, his father had called to ask him his opinion on desktop PCs and now he'd finally gone and bought one.

"Well, when you come back on Monday, you'll have a new job." He'd grown used to Ann's directness and it didn't catch him off guard often, but it did right now.

"What?" Maybe Tricia was right. He should have spoken up sooner about a raise. How mad would she be if they had to call back Joyce-Jill and cancel the cake with the ganache icing? Surely his mom could bake something passable for the reception.

Ann must have seen the terror on his face because she slapped him on the shoulder and laughed. "Don't worry. I'm promoting you to project manager. That comes with a little raise, too. University still has a tight hold on the budget for this department, but I squeezed some more out of them. You've been working hard. You deserve it."

Gordon relaxed in his chair and let out a breath. A raise? This was excellent news. Tricia would be thrilled. "Thank you. You had me worried for a second."

"You didn't think I'd ever let you go, did you? You've been invaluable."

Gordon chuckled. "I've loved working on this project."

"I've got a list of departments that need help after we finish with Payroll, so you'll be busy. But I'm bringing on a couple more programmers, so that will help. I'll need you to visit with each department. Spend time learning their processes and see what needs they have."

Gordon nodded.

"But don't be afraid to make your own suggestions. You've got a good sense for this stuff. Payroll never would have come up with that dashboard the way you did."

This was sounding better and better. This job was basically what he'd been doing in his head with the bakery and dozens of other businesses and university departments over the last few months.

Ann pushed a piece of paper across the desk. "Starting Monday, this will be your new salary."

Gordon flipped over the paper. It wasn't a windfall, but it was definitely a step in the right direction. He couldn't wait to see the look on Tricia's face when he told her.

"I'll expect you to help define and run the projects. You'll be working closely with the two new programmers."

"Of course." Gordon's mind spun with ideas for how he'd organize and track new projects, and he didn't want to wait until Monday to start. He wanted to start right away.

* * *

Summer sun streamed through the kitchen window of Gordon and Tricia's tiny apartment. "I've got an appointment with the head of the biology department this morning." Gordon finished making his peanut butter sandwich, tucked it in a zip top, and tossed it in his shoulder bag.

"I've got an interview with that call center for the HR job at one," Tricia said between sips of coffee, "and then I need to swing by the photography studio to pick up the proofs from the wedding photos. We can look at them tonight when you get home and pick out the ones we want." Tricia rinsed out her mug, stuck it upside down in the dishrack and turned sideways to scoot around him in their narrow kitchen.

"If you can drop me off at the life science building, you can have the car for the day." When Gordon's Toyota Celica had conked out just past Cheyenne after a weekend visit to the farm and the local mechanic wanted a small fortune to fix it, Gordon decided it was time to let the old car go. Tricia's Honda was only two years old and she was still making payments on it. When they looked at their finances, a new car, even a used one, just wasn't an option.

"Sounds good," Tricia said.

"I can probably get a ride home from Carlos, so you won't have to worry about picking me up."

Tricia pulled the ironing board out of the tiny closet in the front room and extended it to its full height, bending over to plug the iron into the wall. "Oh, I forgot to tell you. We got a letter from the property management company." She walked to the stack of bills and junk mail piled up next to the answering machine and grabbed the envelope on top. "Rent is going up at the start of fall semester."

"That's like two months." Gordon imagined their monthly budget on a spreadsheet and imagined making adjustments to the cell for their rent money and watching the negative number pop up on the bottom line. Where else could they cut back?

"I should have a job soon," Tricia said, running the iron back and forth over her interview blouse. "That will help."

"What about our plan to save your salary for a down payment on a house?"

"Well, we'd still be saving most of it."

That might push them back from home ownership by a year *if* they didn't absolutely have to buy a second car and *if* the rent didn't go up again, and *if* there weren't unexpected medical bills. And all of this was of course contingent on *if* Tricia got this job. That was too many ifs. "Let's talk about it tonight. We have time. Maybe we can look for another place to rent?"

Tricia nodded and draped her blouse over a hanger and hung it off the closet door frame. "Ready to go?" she asked, and Gordon nodded, slinging his bag over his shoulder.

On the drive, they took turns pointing out possible apartment buildings they could move to and Tricia said she would make some phone calls when she got home and ask about prices for one-bedrooms. "Don't worry," Gordon said when she pulled up in front of the life sciences building. "We'll work everything out. Just focus on nailing your interview." He leaned across the gear shift and kissed her.

"Thanks," she smiled.

Gordon took the steps two at a time and made his way through the halls to Shannon Chamber's office. He'd spent a few weeks interviewing the professors and other staff in the biology department about what they needed for their ecosystems modeling program. Gordon had already given some preliminary instructions to the programmers, and they had a good start, but they would need to start building in specific requirements. For that, Gordon needed to chat with Shannon.

This project was so much different than the tax updates he'd written into the payroll system and the change of focus was invigorating. Each project was like a new puzzle to solve. He had to find out what all the pieces were, organize them, and then put them together in the right order. His mind was constantly challenged and his creativity tested in exciting ways every single day. He was reminded again as he spoke with Shannon how glad he was that he hadn't gone home to work on the farm.

Still, he'd only gotten his promotion and raise six months ago and already it seemed like it wasn't enough. What did project managers in other places normally make? Was it more? Less?

He walked back to his office in the computer science building and got to work, becoming so absorbed that the day slipped away. Gordon even worked through lunch, eating his peanut butter sandwich at his desk. Completely unaware of the time, he was surprised to look up and see Tricia.

"I've been standing here for two minutes. I can't believe you didn't see me."

Gordon's mind took a second to switch from code to the reality of his new wife standing in front of him. "I thought I told you I'd get a ride home from Carlos. You didn't have to come pick me up."

"I know. I wanted to have dinner with you." She held up an insulated bag and two beers. "Besides, I think Carlos left a half hour ago."

Gordon looked at his watch. How was it six o'clock already?

"What's the occasion?" He wasn't a suspicious man, but he could tell something was up.

"No occasion." Tricia grabbed Gordon by the hand and pulled him up. "Come on. I know there's a little table out in the courtyard and it's a nice evening."

"Fine, I guess I could use the break." Gordon quickly saved his work and logged out but that niggling feeling that Tricia was hiding something wouldn't let go. When he sat at the outdoor picnic table and Tricia pulled out two chicken salad sandwiches, Gordon demanded answers.

"Out with it. I know there's something you want to say. Is this about the interview? Did it go well?"

"It was fine, but I'm not sure that's the job for me."

"What? But we really could use the money. What didn't you like about it?" Tricia's job search seemed to be moving at a glacial pace and it was painful to get so close, only to have to go back and start at square one, looking for somewhere else to apply.

"I was kind of thinking I should start looking for work in Oregon." Her wry smile teased him, so he teased back.

"So, you're leaving me after just two months of marriage? That's rude."

Tricia swatted him on his arm. "No. I thought you could get a job in Oregon, too." She pulled a folded-up piece of paper from her pocket and flattened it in front of him. "I saw it at the student center at C4C. Pulled it right off the wall and made a photocopy at the copy center."

"Mama Meg's Cookie Company in Portland, Oregon, seeks business analyst/project manager," he read.

"That's what you do, right?" Tricia's look was cautiously excited.

"Yes. But why would we move to Oregon? I thought you liked Denver. It's close to family."

"Denver is great, but I heard Oregon is beautiful." She lingered on the word beautiful as she flipped the flyer over. The starting salary was listed at the bottom and Gordon blinked a couple times to make sure he saw it correctly. Yep. Nearly twice as much as he was making with the university. He looked at Tricia and saw her eyes full of light and hope. "You can do this."

He pulled the sheet toward him and reviewed the required experience and skills. Yeah, he definitely could do it, but moving 1200 miles away? Leaving Ann? She was the one who'd seen his potential and offered him something besides working on the farm. Her mentorship was a gift he didn't think he could ever repay. A stab of loyalty shot through him, as if wanting to pin him down to this place forever.

"Just mail them your resume," Tricia said. "If they want to interview you, you can talk to Ann then."

Gordon considered this. There was no harm in sending a resume. Tricia was right. Chances are they wouldn't even call him. Then he wouldn't have to tell Ann and feel disloyal.

But if he did get an interview, and if they did offer him that job, that salary would make a huge difference for them. Homeownership might be cut down to mere months instead of years in the future. They could buy a second car and still have plenty saved in an emergency account.

"Doesn't it rain a lot in Portland?" Gordon asked, giving Tricia one more chance to express any kind of hesitancy.

"I love rain."

Gordon picked up the paper for one last look, then carefully re-folded it and put it in his shirt pocket. "Fine, then. I'll send a resume tomorrow."

Chapter 3
October 1994

"Stop!" Tricia demanded. "That one's for sale. I want to grab the flyer."

Gordon pulled over to the curb and Tricia ran out into the constant drizzle that hadn't let up since they'd arrived in Portland three weeks earlier. She didn't even bother pulling up the hood of her raincoat. She was acclimating to the damp weather much faster than he was. After coworkers had given him a hard time when they'd seen him crossing the parking lot at Mama Meg's with an umbrella, Gordon figured he'd better get used to getting wet.

Tricia jumped back in the car, water droplets jumping from her coat to everything Gordon touched. "Two bedroom, two bathroom. This is such a cute neighborhood. And it's in our price range."

"Our price range?" Gordon said. "We couldn't even come close to the twenty percent down payment. Besides, don't you think this neighborhood is a little weird?"

Tricia wiggled out of her wet coat and pushed it to the floor. "First, we don't have to have twenty percent. That's why they have mortgage insurance. And with my salary plus yours, we'll be able to get rid of that in no time. Second, the neighborhood isn't weird. It's *charming*."

Gordon entered the roundabout in the center of the neighborhood and tried another one of the streets that spoked off in another direction. The neighborhood plat was like a giant wagon wheel with this rose garden at the center. Except right now, it was just a bunch of scraggly canes. He imagined it might be beautiful in a few months, but for now, it looked uninviting at best.

"There's another one!" Tricia jumped out into the rain and returned with another flyer. "Ooh, a breakfast nook. Doesn't that sound nice?"

They'd driven around Portland looking for homes for the last three weekends and some weeknights, too, if Gordon got home in time.

"Who names a neighborhood Ladd's Addition? What does that even mean?" Gordon said.

"Who cares what it means? It's right in the middle of my job and yours. We'd each only have about a fifteen-minute commute. It's perfect."

"I still think we should wait a few months. Save some money. The apartment's pretty nice, don't you think?"

Tricia shrugged. "I guess. But what happens if we wait for six months and then prices go up? I think it makes sense to buy now."

Gordon pulled into the parking lot of Burgerville, a regional chain that everyone at work seemed to think was the only acceptable place to get burgers. Maybe some hand cut fries and a seasonal pumpkin spice milkshake would take Tricia's mind off home buying for a while. There were just too many unknowns for him to make a decision about it now. They hadn't even looked at neighborhoods on the other side of the river, where lots of new construction was happening.

Tricia grabbed her folder of all the home sale flyers she'd collected the last three weeks and stuffed it in her purse. "We can go over these while we eat." She smiled and wiggled her eyebrows like she was being clever.

Gordon only felt stressed.

* * *

Monday morning, a note on Gordon's desk instructed him to check in with his boss, Raheem.

"We've been summoned," he said good naturedly from behind his two computer monitors. "Walt's got a project for us and Jack needs to be brought in on it, so we've got to head up there this morning and see what's up."

Walt was the CFO of Mama Meg's, so Gordon figured it probably had something to do with company finances. Jack, on the other hand, was the president, so whatever this problem was, it was probably a big one.

They met in Jack McCallister's office, a sort of museum of Mama Meg's past advertising campaigns. Framed posters lined the walls going all the way back to the first flyers Meg had passed out to friends and coworkers when she had started her cookie baking business out of her kitchen in the '70s. "Hey, Gordon. How have your first few weeks been?" Jack stretched back in his chair and gestured for Gordon and the others to take a seat.

"Really good." Gordon sank into the leather club chair, instantly at ease in the president's office. Margaret, Meg, McCallister, Jack's mom, was CEO and a more intimidating figure, at least from what Gordon could tell. He tried to square the image of the sweet, aproned mother pulling cookies from an oven in some of the earlier advertising with the imposing, sixty-something woman who commanded respect from everyone, from manufacturing all the way to the C-Suite.

"You know about free cookie Friday, right?" Walt said. "Raheem conveniently forgets to mention that to new hires." He shot the IT manager a sly grin.

"I was getting to it," Raheem said with an air of feigned offense.

When he saw Gordon's confused expression, Jack explained. "Basically, we put a few cases in the breakroom once or twice a month and employees can grab a couple packages to bring home."

"That sounds great," Gordon said. "I might need to start riding my bike to work to make up for the extra calories, but it will be worth it."

"Well, if you do, you'll be in good company. We have quite a few bike commuters on staff." Jack smiled.

"Before we get too distracted by cookies," Walt said, "let's talk about the problem we're having."

Gordon flipped open his notebook and readied his pen.

"We've got a big problem with wastage. Right now, we're tossing hundreds of pounds of perishable ingredients every month because they expire before we use them." Walt leaned forward and planted his elbows on his knees. "We're also having to toss unsold product. Manufacturing says it's purchasing's fault because they order more ingredients than are needed, but purchasing says they're just working off the sales numbers. Of course, the sales department has their own reasons for the way they make projections."

Gordon nodded as he wrote.

"I need you to find out what's going on, where the breakdown in our process is, and figure out how to fix it. This is literally money we are throwing away and our quarterly numbers are taking a hit." Walt flexed his hands and clenched them, like the thought of losing so much money was causing him physical pain.

"We've got to get it under control now, or it's going to mess with our financial goals for the year," Jack added.

"We'll need to talk to each of the departments and learn how the cookies are made, start to finish, if we're going to flush out the problem," Raheem said. "Gordon, that will be your job."

"I've already let everyone know you'd be contacting them. They'll be expecting you," Walt said.

"Got it. I'll start on this immediately," Gordon said.

"Good." Jack relaxed slightly, leaning back in his chair again. "Because I need this turned around by fourth quarter. That will give you about eight months to diagnose, find a solution, implement it, and then get results."

That timeline was going to be tight and for a second, Gordon felt the pressure of this new job with its nice salary and wondered if he was up for the challenge. This was much bigger than his last job, and the stakes were higher. What if he couldn't find the problem in time? Or what if he got it wrong and his recommendation didn't solve the problem? He took a deep breath and remembered Ann's words of encouragement when he told her about this job. She'd been sorry to see him leave CU but knew this was the perfect next step for his career. More than that, she'd told him he was ready. He *was* ready for this challenge.

"We'll look at the findings together," Raheem said to Gordon. "And of course, if you need any help, come to me."

"I'm on it," Gordon said.

"Perfect," Jack said. Walt nodded and Raheem stood. The meeting was apparently over. Gordon took his cue and Raheem headed back to the IT department to get started.

* * *

Gordon's first stop was to Chris, the manufacturing manager down on the production floor. Except for the rhythmic thrum of packaging machines, which built to a crescendo the closer he got to Chris's office, Gordon thought it wouldn't be so bad to work down here with the constant smell of fresh-baked cookies. Chris led Gordon back to his office and shut the door, muting most of the machine noise.

"Listen," Chris said. "I want to eliminate waste as much as Walt does. It kills me to dump so much stuff." He ran his hand over his thick brown beard. "But I'm not the one buying ingredients. Purchasing makes those decisions based on sales projections. They've got contracts that were drawn up months ago and I realize it's not so nimble that we can just change an order at the last minute."

"Can't you use up the ingredients at the end of the month? You could make extra product and that would use up all the extra ingredients, and you'd be ahead on filling orders because cookies would already be made."

"It's not that simple," Chris said. "Making cookies is a fixed process. There's no real way to speed it up. We only have a certain number of machines to do the mixing, shaping, and baking. Jobs get scheduled out each week so we use everything efficiently. We can't just throw another batch in the oven. We would need several extra days at the end of the month to do that and that would bump our labor costs."

Gordon nodded and made a few notes on a notepad.

"The other problem is that we may have five hundred pounds of egg product expiring and only a few bags of sugar. So, even if we had the time to make extra cookies, we don't have excess of all the ingredients we'd need to make the cookies." Chris plopped a four-inch three-ring binder on the table and flopped it open, swiping past recipes in plastic page protectors before landing on one called Monkey Bars. "We made this one last month and ended up with several hundred pounds of left-over banana puree, but we didn't have the walnuts and would have quickly run out of these other ingredients." He ran his finger down the page. "We could have short ordered, but that's the most expensive way to purchase, and since there wasn't an open order for this product, it might have sat on the shelf beyond our freshness guarantee period. We could have had our salespeople push the cookies to their customers, or even offered a discount to move them, but we're already through the roof on the overhead because we would have overpaid for the ingredients. We paid the employees who had to make them. We used up packaging to pack them. And ultimately, we may just have to toss them or donate them. It's cheaper just to toss the extra product."

"I see." Gordon had not even considered the cost of using unneeded product. This was definitely more complicated than he'd imagined.

"There's also a huge cost involved in breaking down a production line and setting it up again for a new cookie," Chris said. "Why don't I give you a tour of the whole line and you can see for yourself?"

Gordon took careful notes while Chris showed him where the product came in, how it was stored, and how it was combined with other ingredients to make a wide variety of cookies. Huge refrigerators stored pallets of boxes full of perishable ingredients, and Gordon shivered as Chris pointed out all the different ingredients and when they would expire. Thousands of dollars worth of product were stored here. Gordon needed to work fast to solve this problem before they had to dump it all.

He spent the next week learning how the shipping department took the finished cookies and packaged and shipped them. He met with the supply chain manager who told him about the contracts they had with wheat and sugar cane growers and how their purchases were based on forecasting not just weather, but what the crop yield would be. At the end of each day, Gordon entered his written notes on a document in his computer and used a spreadsheet to track and organize the data he was collecting. Before long, he had a pretty clear picture of how a Mama Meg's cookie went from farm to store shelf. But he still couldn't see how to effectively reduce waste. He'd planned to take a week to diagnose the problem, and then another week to draft his solution, and then the rest of the time to implement it so that he could meet Jack's timeline, but he was already behind schedule.

The problem consumed him and he found it hard to stop rearranging the pieces of the puzzle in his mind, searching for a solution, even when he got home. He'd picked up some take-out from a Korean restaurant near their apartment on his way home and was still going over the facts and data as he dug into his bibimbap across the table from Tricia.

"Are you even listening to me?"

Gordon looked up to see Tricia looking annoyed.

"Sorry, this thing from work is bugging me." Gordon took a bite of rice and egg that had a little bit too much hot sauce and reached for his water. He swallowed. "What were you saying?"

"I was saying that Julie from the accounting department across the hall from me just bought a house on the west side. It's a new construction and she said there are still lots for sale. Maybe we should go look this weekend?" Tricia looked at him with eyes full of hope that made Gordon regret what he said even before the words even left his mouth.

"I can't. I have to work."

"On Saturday? And Sunday?" Tricia let her fork hang in the air, a bite of rice and kimchi stuck to the tines.

Gordon felt guilty about working instead of spending time with his wife, but his anxiety about getting to the bottom of the waste issue was calling the shots. "This project is really important to the company. They're counting on me. If I mess this up, I may not have a job." Gordon knew this wasn't true, but it accurately reflected the gravity of the situation as far as he was concerned. Tricia's eyes widened and she set down her fork, her rice and kimchi momentarily forgotten. "No job, no house," he said.

Tricia sighed. "It's really that serious?"

"It is for Mama Meg's. This is tens of thousands of dollars per month we're talking about." Gordon took a bite of rice. The fact was, it was not a good idea to buy a house until they had at least a twenty percent down payment. Maybe it was his careful, Midwest thriftiness coming out, but all of Tricia's insistence that they get a house now had bothered him from the start. And yeah, maybe he was using this project at work as an excuse to avoid telling Tricia how he really felt, but figuring out how to fix the waste problem was important and for now, it would do nicely as a reason to put off looking for a house.

"Okay," Tricia said. "I guess you need to work then. I'll just do something else on Saturday." She studied her bibimbap, mixing it up before finally taking a bite. Her voice was understanding, but her slumped shoulders and suddenly sober mood showed her dejection.

"Once the project is finished, things will ease up and we'll start looking again," Gordon said. He knew he was delaying the conversation they needed to have, but he hated seeing her upset.

"That's fine," Tricia said. "I get it. This is important. You need to focus for now. There will still be homes for sale in a few months." She smiled and carried the used takeout containers to the trash, before changing the subject to whether he wanted popcorn or a slice of cake while they watched *Mad About You* and *Friends*.

* * *

Nancy, Mama Meg's sales manager, attempted to angle her monitor so Gordon could see it, but the CRT would only swing around so much. Gordon shifted his chair to the side of her desk and followed her finger as she went over the sales numbers. "These accounts are our regulars. They've placed consistent orders for the last twelve quarters and I'd put money on them doing the same for the next quarter." She clicked a tab and a new spreadsheet popped up. "These customers are hit or miss. Some of them are growing quickly, so we have to look at those numbers to determine what kind of sales to project. Others are getting smaller and...you know the drill. We project fewer sales for them. It's more of an art than a science."

Well, that's one problem, Gordon thought.

"We've actually been pretty accurate with our sales forecast, though, so I'm not sure what the problem with manufacturing is." Nancy clicked another tab and a new spreadsheet popped up. "Here's the projected sales in column B, and the actual sales in C, with the difference here, in D."

She was right. They were usually off by more than 50 units a month. Gordon didn't see a connection between sales projections and manufacturing's wastage. What would he tell Jack if he couldn't find anything?

Then he saw it.

"Wait a second," Gordon said just before Nancy clicked away. "You've grouped the projections by quarter."

"That's right."

"But you're giving purchasing projections for three quarters at a time, right? Nine months?"

"No. We only project our sales out three months. Why?"

This was it! This was what he'd been looking for. "Ingredients like flour and sugar have to be ordered nine months in advance," he explained, "when the wheat and cane sugar are still in the ground. That's why the ingredients aren't matching up with sales forecasts. They're making their nine month purchasing projections based on your three-month sales projections."

"That makes sense," Nancy said."

Gordon felt a surge of energy. "I've got to bring Chris into this. Mind if I give him a call?" Now that he knew the problem, he was ready to come up with solutions.

Chris was available and came right up to Nancy's office. In fact, he was there so quickly, he still had his beard net on. "What did you find out?" he asked, pulling the facial hair covering off, wadding it up, and shoving it in his pocket.

Gordon explained, "You guys are doing your best to use the ingredients efficiently, but because you've got nine months of ingredients and three months of sales projections, you sometimes make products that don't sell. Other times you have leftover ingredients you can't use."

Chris stroked his beard as he considered this, while Nancy nodded. "So, what you're saying if we can get a sales forecasting method that aligns more closely with the manufacturing supply chain constraints, we could cut waste?"

"Exactly," Gordon said.

"How about we go over a few options right now," Nancy said. "I can run them past my sales team. If they don't see any problems, I'll implement it immediately and send the new numbers to purchasing."

Chris beamed. "Perfect."

* * *

Glasses clinked at the bar and a low din of conversation filled the corner bistro while white-aproned waiters zipped from table to table. "What did Jack say when he saw the numbers?" Tricia asked, taking a sip of wine.

"Well, they cut the waste down by half. Obviously, he was thrilled."

"That's great, honey. I knew you'd figure it out."

Gordon sipped from his glass. He'd splurged on a bottle of wine—not the most expensive on the menu, of course, but still more than he'd ever spent for wine. It was more than worthy of tonight's celebration.

"Now we can get back to looking for a house," Tricia said, excitedly. Gordon half expected her to produce her folder of flyers, but he was fairly certain the tiny evening bag she'd brought with her wasn't big enough to hold it.

He thought about letting it go...about kicking the conversation down the road just one more time. This was a celebration, after all, and what was wrong with enjoying the evening? But he was exhausted from avoiding this conversation, from feigning interest on their weekend drives, and from the guilt of not being honest. He'd just saved Mama Meg's fifty thousand dollars a quarter. He could talk to his wife.

He inhaled and exhaled. "About house hunting," he started.

Tricia's expression of delight froze and fear settled into the lines around her eyes. She'd been patient for so long. He'd still see the occasional real estate flier sticking out of her purse, but in the eight months he'd worked on the project for Walt and Jack, she'd never brought up homebuying once. At the same time, their commitment to bag lunches and cheap dates eating microwave popcorn with a movie checked out from the library had paid off. Their savings account had ballooned. Maybe they were ready?

Gordon smiled and Tricia's expression relaxed. Finally, he spoke. "I think it's time we get a real estate agent."

Tricia squealed as she reached out and grabbed his hand across the table and gave it a squeeze.

Chapter 4
January 1996

Rain had been Gordon's constant commute companion since mid-October, except for those two days in December when it snowed, covering the ground with an inch of fluffy white stuff and bringing the city to a halt. What would his friends back in Denver say if they saw the miles of traffic parked on I-5 and the abandoned cars stuck in the center median strip, all for a little dusting? As crazy as it might have been, he didn't mind the snow days with Tricia, snug in their new house, sipping cocoa and watching an X-Files marathon.

His commute from Portland's west side to Tualatin wasn't too bad, but as he focused on the rain-blurred taillights in front of him, he had serious thoughts about investing in some high-performance windshield wipers.

At Mama Meg's, Gordon greeted the receptionist as he scanned his badge, letting it retract on the chain he wore at his hip. After a year and a half working for the cookie company, Gordon finally felt settled. He understood the business, knew all the players, and had made some great friends in the process. His relationship with Raheem had been especially fulfilling. On the most hectic, stressful days, he always looked forward to working through problems with his boss and mentor. Raheem challenged him to think about IT solutions in new ways, motivated him to stay up to date on the latest trends, and was a sounding board when he needed to talk through things, both work and personal.

He greeted several people he passed in the hallway on the way to his office and passed the bank of cubicles that housed the customer service team. Over the tops he had a clear view to Jack's office in the front corner. The president was usually easy going and good natured, and Gordon smiled thinking about how that persona grew slightly more serious whenever his mother was around. Just as he rounded the corner, something made him look back to Jack's office. The door that just moments before had been closed, was now open. He saw Jack, pumping Raheem's hand as they paused at the threshold, half in, half out.

Had there been a meeting this morning he didn't know about? No, he was sure Raheem would have reminded him if it was something he needed to attend. Gordon let the scene slip from his mind, switching to the list of tasks that he had to get done today. Walt had been pushing to upgrade the purchase order system by bringing in an Electronic Data Interchange module for their ERP system. A lot of their bigger customers were starting to request vendors get the EDI module to make ordering streamlined and trackable. It was a good move and would make things a lot easier for Mama Meg's in the long run, but it would be expensive and the roll out would be complicated. They were poised to start, though, as soon as Jack and Meg gave the go ahead.

He'd just powered up his computer and started organizing his tasks for the day when Raheem popped his head in his office.

"You get those specs Walt sent over?" he said.

Gordon held up the file folder as confirmation. "It's at the top of my to-do list," he said.

"Great." Raheem took a seat in Gordon's extra chair and threaded his fingers together in his lap, pausing for just a beat before continuing to speak. "I wanted you to be one of the first to know. I just came from Jack's office," he started.

If there was a corporate world version of fight or flight, Gordon was feeling it now. His senses heightened in anticipation, readying himself for a blow.

"I've given my two weeks' notice. I've got a great job as IT Director at a start-up in Seattle." Raheem's face said all Gordon needed to know. He was thrilled about his new opportunity. "I'm getting in on the ground floor."

"Wow." He let the word hang for a few seconds, hoping it would fill up the space until he knew what to say. A stampede of thoughts rushed through his head. What was he going to do without his friend? Who would be his next boss? Would he get along with him as well as he'd gotten on with Raheem?

"A recruiter called, actually. I wasn't actively looking. But the opportunity...it was too good to pass up."

"I'll miss working with you, man," Gordon said, finally. "But I'm excited for you." Still, questions flowed more freely than anything helpful or kind he could actually say to Raheem. What about the EDI project Walt was gearing up for? There was no way he'd be able to do it without Raheem, was there?

"Thanks. And hey, just so you know, Jack and Walt are going to start looking for a replacement right away, but I did give them one person's name as a recommendation." Raheem smiled, conspiratorially.

"Who?" Gordon asked, wondering if he'd like the suggestion. He could easily think of a few people he hoped it was not.

Raheem shook his head and laughed. "You, of course."

"Me?" Gordon's brain struggled to keep up with this new information. Forgotten were his concerns from just moments earlier. Now he wondered if he was ready for the responsibility.

"You'd have to interview, go through the whole process, but yes, you. You'd make a great IT manager."

"Thanks," Gordon said.

"Of course. And hey, I'll just be a phone call away if you need advice or just want to chat. And I fully expect a call whenever you find yourself up my way."

Gordon smiled and nodded, feeling the tether to his boss and friend, that had moments ago broken, reform itself with tenuous but real links. "You're going to a start-up," he said. "You're not going to have time to take my calls. You'll be lucky if you have time to pee."

"True," Raheem admitted, chuckling to himself. "Still, don't be a stranger. I'm serious."

"You got it," Gordon replied, already planning to talk to Tricia about a weekend get-away as soon as he got home.

* * *

The promotion to IT manager happened fast. Gordon wasn't even sure they interviewed any outside candidates. Mama Meg's, did, however, allow Gordon to hire a couple of new business analysts, and that put Gordon's mind at ease as he readied himself to tackle Walt's new project.

"Several of our suppliers have offered incentives for using EDI transactions," Walt said. Gordon and he were at yet another meeting with Jack and Meg. "Cargill said they'd give us two percent off our first EDI transaction and one percent after that. That could potentially save us four thousand a year, just from our sugar order." Walt threw a bar graph up on the overhead projector. "Eventually, other suppliers will offer similar incentives, so it makes sense to invest the time and money to get it set up now."

Meg and Jack nodded thoughtfully. Since the project was costly and time consuming, they had the final say, but Walt's graphs showing how fast Mama Meg's would recoup the cost of the EDI module looked like it was doing the trick.

"We'll also have the capacity to process orders faster, and as more of our clients get their own EDI systems, efficiency will continue to increase." He switched out transparencies, the new one showing his five-year projection. "There are a lot of factors at play, but it's not unreasonable to believe that with savings and increased business, our revenue in five years could look something like this." Walt pointed with the end of his pen to the bar that soared nearly off the page.

"I like it," Meg said. "How long will it take to get it operational?"

Walt went over the timeline while Gordon made a preliminary list of tasks. He'd have to look at different EDI modules to find one that worked best with their current ERP. He'd need to purchase all the necessary software. He'd have to assign someone to get the module plugged into Mama Meg's system. He'd have to look into the EDI protocols the buyer and supplier were using to ensure their system responded to transactions. He would need to make sure all the communication links were working properly. The more he thought about it, the more he realized how many places the project could go off rails. He'd have to make sure he anticipated every potential for failure and made contingencies.

This was the first major project since Raheem left for Seattle three weeks ago and Gordon felt the pressure to get it right. Walt and Jack had put their faith in him, promoting him to IT manager, and Gordon didn't want to let them down. He felt the urge to call Raheem, to run everything past him and get his opinion and guidance. But his friend was probably busy. Besides, he needed to stand on his own two feet. Certainly he could handle this with Walt and his team.

He returned to his office and pulled in his BAs to make assignments, then started making phone calls and gathering information on EDI systems. He listed out specs in a spreadsheet so he could compare the different modules and then match them up against the accounting department's requirements. But as he got more information, it became clear that this project was way more than simply order taking. It would involve interfacing with the ERP systems their customers used, as well as configuring the EDI component of the ERP system to respond properly to the incoming orders.

He ate lunch at his desk and continued to work, absorbed in researching all the parts of the project. Sometime in the late afternoon his phone rang, startling him. Probably someone returning his call about a module. "This is Gordon," he said.

"Hey, honey."

The greeting caught him off guard and it took him a second to realize it wasn't a salesperson on the other end. "Tricia, hi. What's up?" She hardly ever called him at work and for a moment he wondered if everything was okay.

"Just wondering what time you're coming home tonight," she said.

Gordon leaned back in his chair and stretched his legs, letting out a groan of pleasure. He hadn't realized how much he'd cramped up just sitting in his chair. "I suspect the regular time, why?" The regular time had been about five-thirty, but it was getting a little later every day.

Tricia was quiet for a moment and then spoke. "Gordon, it's eight-thirty."

Eight-thirty? He checked his watch and sure enough, Tricia was right. How come no one else had said anything to him? He wheeled backwards in his chair, the phone cord stretching across the room, so he could look out at his BA's desks. But they were empty, and the halls were quiet. He'd completely lost track of time. "I had no idea it had gotten to be so late."

"Well," Tricia asked, "you coming home now?"

"Yeah." Gordon surveyed his desk, papers spread an inch deep over the entire surface. It would take him at least twenty minutes to get to a point where he could leave. "I just need to wrap things up here and I'll head out."

Thirty minutes later, Gordon found his car in the nearly empty parking lot and headed for home. The EDI project was going to take a huge chunk of his time, but he still had all of his other responsibilities as IT manager, and he wondered how he would get it all done. How had Raheem handled it? Gordon was fairly sure that his old manager had never stayed at work this late. And yet Gordon didn't see how he could keep up with everything without staying late. He'd have to explain it to Tricia when he got home. Things were just going to be busy for a while.

* * *

"Walt," Gordon said. He'd called instead of walked to his office to save time.

"What's up?" Walt said.

"I've been looking at the specs from the ERP vendor and working with the sales team and I've hit a snag."

"Okay. Let's hear it," Walt said.

"This EDI module is going to require us to interface with our customer's ERP systems. We'll have to configure our EDI component of the ERP system to respond properly to the incoming orders." Gordon rubbed his tired eyes and tried to get a handle on the problem so he could explain it best to Walt.

"Hmm."

"The way it's set up," Gordon said, "outgoing EDI transactions will go to suppliers, while incoming will come in from buyers. We're going to wind up with a mishmash of stuff coming in from every direction."

"What's the solution?" Walt asked.

"Our system needs to see the order, then communicate with our suppliers about our needs. It's going to take a lot of reconfiguration."

"Okay," Walt said. "So we have a little more work to do. I can buy us a couple more months. But that's it. After that we've got to get this up and running. This definitely needs to be functional for more than just our biggest client to be profitable."

Gordon had taken to keeping a pillow and blanket in his backseat for naps during his lunch break. His only sustenance during the day came from a box of granola bars under his desk. Tricia kept leftovers in the fridge for him each night, but he usually ate those for breakfast before he slipped out the door. He was getting four to five hours of sleep a night and wasn't sure how much longer this pace was sustainable. He couldn't say no to Walt, though. Gordon was IT manager. He needed to get this done. "Agreed," he finally said. "We'll get it done."

"Great," Walt said. "Are you going to the Society for Information Management meeting Thursday? There might be some people there you can talk to about this. I'm sure they'll have some great advice."

Gordon almost laughed. He didn't have time to go to a meeting. He barely had time to go home. "I don't think I'll make it. Maybe next month." Gordon knew that was a lie. He'd be just as busy next month. Who had time for drinks and socializing when there was so much work to be done?

"Fine, but if I can offer a little advice, you really need to make time for these meetings. They're crucial to building your career."

Had Walt never worked as an IT manager? Did he not know how time consuming and stressful it could be? Getting work done and doing a good job was more crucial to building his career than after-hours schmoozing, he was certain.

"Give me an update in two weeks. I want to make sure we're on track. It's crucial that we get the ERP interface worked out. Got it?"

"Absolutely." Gordon ended the call and let out a long breath, then called his two BAs over to review the game plan. After they left, he made a phone call that he should have made months ago.

"It's great to hear your voice," Raheem said, his every word radiating delight though the phone lines. "How is Mama Meg's treating you?"

"I'll be honest," Gordon said. "It's a little rough right now." He filled Raheem in on the details of the project and their current roadblocks. "I've been working my ass off and we're still having problems."

"I don't envy you," Raheem said. "This is a big task, and not one that I've managed before. Have you had a chance to go to any of the SIM meetings?"

"No." Gordon tried not to let the exasperation come across in his reply. "Walt just suggested that, too, but I just told you I'm working over fourteen hours a day. When would I have time to go to a meeting?

"That's a good point," Raheem admitted. "But you might meet someone at the meeting who's been through a similar set up and configuration. You could get valuable information. It's networking, man. You've got to do it."

"When I have time off from work, I want to go home and see my wife. The last thing I want to do is go to a bar and talk about IT. Besides, I'm networking with you right now."

"Very funny," Raheem said. "Clearly you need to have more than just me in your network. I don't have all the answers, you know."

It felt good to laugh, and really good to talk about something else besides this project, even for a minute.

"You and Tricia need to come up and visit. I'll show you around town. We can make a weekend of it. Maybe catch a Mariners game."

A weekend off. It sounded so nice and yet, out of the question. At least for now. "Maybe in a couple of months, once we get the EDI module up and running and our ERP configured."

"Name the weekend," Raheem said. "You just let me know."

Raheem may not have had the answers he was looking for, but talking with him was the shot in the arm he needed to get back to work. And the promise of a trip north for a visit, a goal he would make sure happened.

* * *

A thick cloud of tension hung over the conference room and matched the dread Gordon felt weighing him down. After the two-month extension and all the late nights, the EDI module was only configured to work with Cargill, their biggest supplier. That was it.

They were able to take advantage of the discount, but even though it was several thousand dollars in savings each quarter, it didn't come close to making up for the investment of time and money spent on the EDI module, the upgrades to the ERP system, and the effort Walt, Gordon, and his team put into the project. Jack was stoic, but Meg looked mad. Gordon wished he could hide.

"I'm going to be blunt," Jack said to Walt and Gordon, "I put this project's failure on both of you."

Gordon couldn't disagree. They'd focused on the accounting department and how the new EDI module would work for them, but they ignored the other departments that would be working with it, assuming that what had worked for accounting would work for all.

How wrong they'd been.

Even with Cargill, the system was still a little buggy and had a tendency to stop working occasionally for no apparent reason, leaving Cargill frustrated as well. Gordon kneaded his brow and wondered if Jack and Meg would fire him right now, in this meeting.

"We made some definite missteps," Walt explained. "But we know now that this needs to be a more organized effort across the company. It's got to be more than just accounting and IT at the table."

Jack nodded.

"This technology is becoming standard in the industry," Meg said. "Adopting it is not in question. We need to move forward with better systems." She turned her gaze first to Walt and then to Gordon, lingering long enough that Gordon struggled not to squirm in his seat. Finally, Meg continued. "I trust you won't make the same mistakes again?"

Gordon felt a rush of relief.

"Absolutely not," Walt assured her.

"Good," Meg said. "Jack." She turned to her son. "I want you to bring in the other executives to the process. If we're going to do this right, we need more voices at the table."

Gordon left the conference room relieved, but exhausted. Tonight, he was definitely leaving at five.

"Gordon."

He turned to see Walt following him and the spring of tension that had just started to uncoil tightened again, ever so slightly. "I'll let you know what I'll need from you after I meet with Jack and the others."

Gordon nodded. "Thanks." His boss could have easily thrown more blame Gordon's way in the meeting. And Gordon might have deserved it. But Walt's shared responsibility was probably the thing that kept him from having to update his resume. There was solace in knowing his boss had his back. He made to leave, but Walt stopped him one more time.

"SIM meets this week. Why don't we go together?"

For the first time that morning, Gordon smiled. "That would be great."

Chapter 5
April 2000

All but two of the school cafeteria tables were folded and shoved up against the walls. The room still smelled of greasy cheese from what Gordon guessed had been *pizza day* on the school lunch menu.

"You need to fill this out with your child's name, age, and shirt size," the cheerful lady behind the table said. "Oh, and if you want to help coach, check this box and write your name and number." Gordon took the paperwork and a pen and moved down the table to another parent volunteer who went over the equipment list: glove, cleats, and a cup.

"It's t-ball. Do they really need a cup?" Gordon asked, a little surprised.

"You'd be surprised," the volunteer dad said, laughing. "Even our four-year-olds can get pretty physical with their game play."

Gordon noticed Tricia pull their son, Jacob, a little closer while a look of concern crossed her face. She'd thought four was probably too young to start team sports, but Gordon looked forward to playing catch and practicing with his little guy.

"It's actually pretty great to watch them get into it," the volunteer said. "It's why I coach. My youngest is on the team this year and I've coached the other two as well. Wouldn't miss this."

"Sounds like fun," Gordon said as he added the equipment list to his pile of papers.

"I'm Darius, by the way." He held out his hand for Gordon to shake. "You thinking of coaching?" Darius raised his brows in question, a sly smile giving away the fact that he was fully in recruiting mode.

"I wish I could," Gordon could feel Tricia watching him. They'd had this conversation several times already. "I'm pretty busy at work these days." He could almost hear his wife rolling her eyes. Busy was an understatement. Most nights he didn't get home until after seven and Tricia had made her feelings about that well known. Darius handed him a copy of the season's practice and game schedule.

"Take a look. A lot of companies cut you some slack if you're volunteering."

Coaching his son in t-ball seemed like an impossible dream. Even if Walt gave him the okay to leave early a few days a week, his workload would continue to grow while he was away from his desk and there would be even more to do when he returned.

"Daddy's going to be my coach?" Jacob said, kicking his legs under the table as they filled out paperwork and wrote checks.

"Daddy's very busy at work," Tricia said, but Jacob had already lost interest in the answer to his question, standing on the bench and walking it like a balance beam. Tricia pulled him down and explained he just needed to be patient for a little longer. "It would be so great if you could, though," she said, wrangling their son into submission in her lap. "I'd feel so much better knowing you were there with him."

"I know." Over the last few years, Gordon's job had turned from its exciting, albeit high pressure, start working on critical business development projects to feeling more like a helpdesk. A very busy, overworked helpdesk. He couldn't help but wonder if it was because of the way he messed up the EDI roll out. Now he was stuck installing software updates, troubleshooting, and working out bugs. Important, sure, but honestly, anyone could have done it.

Jacob had found another little boy and together they freed a couple of red, bouncy playground balls from the cart. Tricia ran to intervene. Gordon's pen hovered over the volunteer check box. Darius seemed like a nice guy and he could see working with him, even as a few kids screamed with joy as they chased each other around the cafeteria in an impromptu game of tag. Then he remembered the grocery store database Marcia in marketing had asked for, and how Chris in manufacturing told him to ignore Marcia's request and see to his system updates first because, he said, *If we don't make cookies, Marcia doesn't have anything to market.*

He skipped over the section about volunteering and signed his name. Maybe one year he'd be able to help coach his son, but this was not that year.

Much later, back home, the phone rang just as Gordon and Tricia were getting ready for bed. It was Walt and immediately, Gordon knew something was wrong. Walt never called him at home. Tricia handed him the cordless phone and he walked into the office, shutting the door behind him.

"Meg went earlier this afternoon."

Went, Walt said, as if she was simply on a business trip, or on a weekend getaway at her beach house. But Gordon knew that's not what he'd meant. Meg's health had been declining for the past year and just a few weeks ago she'd been placed on hospice. The sorrow that tightened around his heart like a vise caught him off guard. Over the last six years, he'd come to respect and admire the figurehead of Mama Meg's cookies. Sure, she was an imposing figure, and Gordon *had* spent his first year trying to avoid passing her in the hallway. But the more he got to know her, the more he saw her indomitable spirit, unlimited energy, quick wit, and exceptionally warm heart.

"Damn," Gordon said. "How are Jack and Laura doing?" Laura, Jack's sister, had joined the company several years back, a solid addition to the executive team.

"As well as can be expected. There will be information about a public memorial service in a few days. It looks like there might be some drama from Scott and Brigitte, but I don't think that will affect us all that much."

Gordon winced. He certainly hoped not. Scott worked in his department and was already enough trouble.

"I'll let you know if anything changes," Walt said. "But for now, business as usual. I just wanted to let you know about Meg."

Gordon thanked him and hung up the phone and went to find Tricia. He suddenly felt the need to talk about the company's late matriarch. To remember her.

"Did I ever tell you about the time Meg caught me eating Oreos in the lunchroom?" Gordon's voice was soft as he crawled into bed. Tricia had already turned out the light, but he was pretty sure she was still awake.

"Mmhmm," she said into her pillow.

Gordon snuggled close and told her the story again, smiling in the dark as he recalled how Meg insisted he toss the cookies into the trash, and replaced them with several packages of her own Choco Creams.

"She was one tough cookie," he mused, and drifted off to sleep.

* * *

The weeks after Meg's funeral had been, as Walt had predicted, business as usual. Gordon continued to barely keep his head above water in the steadily increasing flood of work. Around week three, however, Gordon noticed tension emanating from Jack's office. More than once, he caught Laura leaving Jack's office with a rigid look on her face, a warning to stay away. It would be understandable if Jack were overwhelmed with his new role, but this seemed like something more.

Marketing and Sales had both come to Gordon with special requests and he'd delegated them out to his team. However, a big chunk of his time at work now was trying to manage Jack's brother, Scott. He'd always been a bit of a liability, but since Meg died, sometimes Gordon wondered if he was actually trying to sabotage the IT Department. Worst of all, Scott's antics were affecting morale. He hesitated to complain directly to Jack, but Walt knew exactly what he thought about the situation. *Hang in there*, was the only thing Walt would tell him, but the situation was unsustainable. Something had to change.

"Gordon," Walt called from down the hall. He had an unfamiliar man with him. Someone new for the IT department, maybe? He would take all the help he could get. As the two men got closer, though, Gordon doubted his first impression. With his salt and pepper hair and pressed khakis, this guy didn't look *entry level*. "Glad I caught you," Walt said. He put his hand on the man's shoulder and seemed to nudge him forward. "This is Emmett Trask. He's an IT consultant."

"Nice to meet you." Gordon managed a friendly smile, but alarm bells sounded in his head. Why was he here? Should he be worried? Was he here to critique Gordon's work? Why hadn't he been warned about this?

"Likewise," Emmett said. His smile was relaxed and lacked any hint of intimidation, but Gordon was still suspicious.

"Emmett's here to observe for a few weeks and then he will make some suggestions for how we can improve efficiencies. Mama Meg's is getting ready to scale, and we need to be ready." Walt fumbled with his hands, crossing them in front of him, then shoving them in his pockets, and for the first time, Gordon noticed the strain behind his smile. It was subtle and Gordon wasn't sure what to make of it.

There had been whisperings that Mama Meg's might be in financial trouble, so he supposed it made sense that Jack would try and plug up holes in the dike. "Anything you need from me?" Gordon asked.

"As it turns out," Emmett said, "I was hoping I could chat with you for a bit. Do you have time now?"

Gordon looked at his watch and quickly scoured his brain for anything he could use as an excuse to delay a meeting, but came up empty.

"He's meeting with sales and manufacturing, too," Walt added. "Even marketing."

"That's right," Emmett said. "I'm just trying to get a clear picture of what's going on—where everyone's pain points are.

Gordon definitely had pain points. It sounded like this was normal procedure and he felt some of his concern drain away. Still, Walt's rigid posture and pasted-on smile told Gordon he needed to watch his step with this guy. He sighed. Might as well talk to Emmett and get it over with. "Now works great," he said, and ushered Emmett back to his office.

"I'm eager to hear how things are going in the IT department," Emmett said as he took a seat across from Gordon's desk.

"Busy," Gordon replied. "Always busy."

"What's keeping you so busy?" Emmett asked.

"I'm working on a major project for Marcia in marketing. She's been wanting me to find a national database of grocery store sales and customer information." Gordon took a deep breath and kept going. "The sales department has new phones and laptops and I have to handle all the software upgrades, as well as troubleshooting any problems that crop up. Most of our time is spent maintaining the PCs, servers, and laptops and of course the network that ties them all together." Once Gordon got talking, he found his words started to flow more freely. "I just don't have the resources to keep the infrastructure running and work on installing and maintaining the applications that people need to do their jobs more efficiently."

Emmet nodded and continued to listen while Gordon talked about how Chris had been badgering him to put manufacturing's needs above marketing or sales.

"Do you think it's a staffing issue?" Emmett asked.

"Sometimes it seems like we could never have enough people. Maybe we need to change the way jobs are requested?" Gordon shook his head. "I don't know. It just seems like the work is coming at me from all sides, all at the same time."

"Do you have any ideas for how you might improve the situation?"

Gordon choked out a laugh. "I barely have time to eat lunch, let alone stop and think. I'm worried about my team, though. Most of them are working hard, but how long can they keep this pace? We've got a lot of great employees and I'd hate to lose them because they burned out." There was something therapeutic about voicing his concerns and he felt the smallest weight lift from his shoulders.

"Well," Emmett started, "I can help you right now with the national grocery store database. One of my clients is using—and happy with—this company here." He slid a scrap of paper with a name written on it across the table. "Give them a look. I think they'll be a good fit for Marcia."

"Thanks." Gordon nodded once. Maybe this guy wasn't so bad after all.

"I'm going to be honest with you." Emmett set his pad of paper and pen down and spoke freely. "You need a better understanding of business."

And there it was. This guy was here to shake things up and it appeared Gordon was one of the things he wanted to shake.

"You need to communicate better with department heads. And you need a system in place to prioritize projects."

The urge to defend himself was strong, but Gordon knew Emmett was right. Right on every point.

"That last one isn't entirely your fault," he added. "I'm going to suggest that Walt put an IT governance process in place immediately. That should help."

"I'll take all the help I can get," Gordon admitted. Emmett's criticism was hard to hear, but the thought of getting real solutions was enough motivation to help him shed his ego.

"I'm glad to hear that. Because this company is poised to double in size, and I don't think you've got the skills to run the IT department through that growth."

Ouch. "Now, wait a second." If this guy was going to suggest he be replaced, he had a few things to say. He'd given up a lot to keep this department going. Sure, they were behind on some of their jobs, but they'd get to everything. Eventually. Of course, ten more would come in by the time they accomplished one.

Emmett jumped in. "I'm not saying you shouldn't be IT Manager. I'm just saying you need some mentoring from an IT pro who can give you some help in figuring out how to build business relationships and prioritize projects. And not from Walt. That's why I'm going to recommend Jack bring in a temporary CIO. My colleague, Tom Tseng, has worked with plenty of IT Managers just like you and helped them to turn their IT departments from what is essentially a fix-it shop into a trusted tech advisor."

Gordon was listening.

"Of course, all of this is dependent on Jack signing off, but Mama Meg's can't grow without IT as a partner at the table."

Was that a light at the end of the tunnel Gordon was seeing? He laughed to himself and shook his head, clearing the vision. If it was, it was a very long tunnel. Still, he really liked what he was hearing.

"How soon can we get Tom here?" Gordon asked.

Emmett smiled. "If I can convince Jack this is the way to go, then soon."

* * *

Two weeks later, Tom Tseng swooped into Mama Meg's like a category one hurricane, stirring things up just enough to catch everyone's attention and blowing over corporate culture that was too outdated to withstand his force. It was easy to see why his presence was met with mixed reactions—especially since one of his first recommendations was to fire Scott. Gordon tried not to celebrate openly. But Jack let everyone know that Tom was there to stay, at least until his temporary assignment was over, and that it was in everyone's, and the company's, best interest to work with him.

Gordon didn't need to be convinced. Tom was exactly the advocate he needed.

"Our first big project is to develop a process to get accurate data about product profitability," Tom explained to Gordon.

"But I've got all these open tickets from just about every department. Shouldn't we take care of those first?" Gordon said.

"Don't worry about those. The steering committee has prioritized the projects, and this is the one they've decided is most important. All the rest can wait."

"Does Leslie know? And Chris?" Gordon was not entirely convinced.

"They're on the steering committee. They're the ones who made the call." Tom's eyebrows danced like he'd just revealed the secret of the universe. And in a way, he kind of had.

"So, the steering committee prioritizes IT projects?"

"Yep. And you need to start coming to meetings with me. We need your input to make the best decisions."

Tom had spent his first weeks in every department at Mama Megs, but now he spent almost half of his time with Gordon. It was immediately clear that Tom was more than interim CIO; he was there to mentor and coach, as well.

"If my recommendations are implemented, we'll get a managed services provider to take over some of the more basic IT tasks, like software updates and help desk calls. That will free up the IT department to focus on projects that actually contribute to the growth of the company."

Gordon's mind reeled. Would outsourcing those tasks really work? It sounded like a dream. Although, he wouldn't mind not running around every day like a chicken with its head cut off. Maybe he would even have time to coach t-ball next season?

* * *

"Way to hustle!" Gordon shouted from the bleachers as Jacob scooped up a grounder and threw it to first, just as he and Gordon had practiced.

"Good job, sweetie!" Tricia called out and Gordon shot her a pointed look.

"You can't call him sweetie in front of his teammates," he said. "They'll make fun of him."

"Oh, they will not." Tricia slapped his arm playfully.

Unfortunately, in his excitement and making the play, Jacob put a little too much muscle into his throw and the ball sailed over the first baseman's head and bounced off the chain link fence. The first baseman then overthrew to second and the ball rolled past a player sitting in left field who seemed to be watching a ladybug crawl on a blade of grass. Darius shouted encouragement to his team from the dugout and parents joined in, even as the runner rounded third and headed toward home. Kids in light blue uniforms skittered around the outfield like bugs under a just-lifted log, lobbing the ball wildly in their efforts to make the play.

It was the first game Gordon had been able to attend all season and, he hoped, not the last. Tom had only been acting CIO for a month, but already Gordon was able to see how the changes he'd recommended were making a positive difference for the company. The biggest difference as far as Gordon was concerned was hope. Hope, and a new vision for his future.

Ever since the governance team and steering committee had started meeting, he saw how technology decisions could be made with focus on strategy rather than the squeaky wheel. He wanted to know more about what it took to be a CIO and he knew that Tom would be able to help guide him.

When they had some time on Monday, Gordon broached the subject. "I'm starting to see the value of technology as an important strategic tool for growth and I want to have more of a seat at the table. I want to know about the path from IT Manager to CIO."

"That's great," Tom said, "because IT has turned a corner and companies that view it as nothing more than a glorified geek squad are going to be left behind. IT managers who truly understand the value of IT and know how to harness its power are the ones who are going to get a seat in the executive suite. Those are the ones who will be in high demand."

Gordon liked the sound of that.

"You've seen what I've done in this first month." Tom ticked off his fingers. "You need to be aware of how technology project decisions are made. That's governance."

Gordon nodded. He'd been brought into these meetings with the heads of every department. Just listening to the needs of each department helped him, and the others, to see how their needs were actually interconnected. New software in the sales department directly affected manufacturing. Similarly, an efficient manufacturing line made a difference in purchasing. It was crucial, therefore, for everyone to be part of the process.

"Next, you need to be aware of how projects are organized," Tom continued. "Projects should be owned by an executive, with IT acting as an advisor. Ownership of the project gets decided and agreed upon through governance." Tom paused to make sure Gordon was following. He was.

"The third thing is organization. You need to know how IT can develop the credibility to become the trusted advisor in the C-Suite."

"What does that look like?" Gordon asked. Ever since they outsourced the helpdesk requests, things in IT had gotten a lot more manageable. But Gordon wasn't sure that was the organization that Tom was talking about.

"Outsourcing more routine responsibilities ..." Tom started, stopped, started again. "Think of that as the first step. That's you, putting on your oxygen mask first before assisting others, so to speak. You can't be helpful unless you've got your own department in order."

"That makes sense," Gordon said. "I have much more time to focus on other departments now that I'm not worrying so much about my own."

"Exactly," Tom brightened. "That's the next step. Focusing on the internal process. Now you strengthen your relationship with each of the departments within Mama Meg's. You get to know about their business, their processes and struggles so that you can better provide better technology solutions."

Gordon thought back to his days at CU and how he couldn't even begin to come up with technology solutions until he truly understood his customer. It was no different now, but his customers were Chris in manufacturing, Leslie in sales, Marcia in marketing as well as the leads in finance and purchasing.

"The last layer in this process is to look outward to Mama Meg's customers and determine how their needs can be met better with technology. That's when IT provides a strategic competitive advantage."

"Kind of like when we brought in the EDI module several years back." Gordon hoped Tom hadn't heard about what a disaster the initial roll-out had been, but he was pretty sure this was the kind of thing Tom was talking about. "Cargill wanted us to start using it to make purchasing easier, and it has."

"You've got it," Tom said. "These three layers, IT infrastructure, internal trust and development, and external focus and strategic development, build on each other and only work if the layer underneath is solid. Kind of like a pyramid. In fact, that's why it's called the IT Pyramid."

"Makes sense." Gordon leaned back in his chair and marveled to himself that there was ever a moment when he didn't trust this man. He'd learned more in the last month with Tom than he had in the last three years with Walt. Not that the CFO was entirely at fault. His specialty was finance, not IT.

Walt should have been glad that Tom was there helping Gordon strengthen his IT skills. However, it seemed the opposite was true. Gordon had to admit the signs were subtle, but he'd worked closely with Walt for six years and could tell when something was off. And when it came to Walt, something was definitely off.

Chapter 6

"I just don't see it," Gordon held his slender flip phone in the palm of his hand at the pop-up bar in the brightly lit hotel conference room. "Even if Wireless Access Protocol was improved, I can't imagine that it would ever allow browsing on my phone like I do on my desktop." Next to him stood Hank Glennon, a Tektronix engineer who had been the night's speaker at their Society for Information Management (SIM) meeting.

"That's why we have to get away from WAP and move to a system that supports HTML," Hank said excitedly. "And it's coming. Soon, you'll be able to have dedicated applications that let customers place orders directly from their phones." His hands flew about dramatically. "Salespeople will be able to connect with their ERP in real time so they can update sales numbers on the road."

It was nearly impossible not to get caught up in Hank's enthusiasm and Gordon took a minute to imagine what that future might look like.

"One day, this will be the only thing we carry. We will use it to pay people, to watch movies, even pre-order a meal at a restaurant so it's ready right when we arrive."

Gordon smirked. "Yeah, but will it still make phone calls?"

Hank chuckled, "Just you wait." He took a sip of his drink and swallowed, arching his brows conspiratorially. "By 2025, we may even be communicating telepathically. No need for phones at all." He finished his drink in one last, long pull, then laughed when he saw Gordon's stunned expression. "Okay, *that* was a joke," he admitted.

"What are you two laughing about?" Tom said, joining them.

"Just speculating about the future," Gordon said.

"Listen," Hank reached into his wallet and produced his card. "Any time you want to chat about it, give me a call."

Gordon thanked him and tucked the card into his shirt pocket. "Or," he said, "I could wait a few years and just…" He tapped his temple and winked.

Hank nodded conspiratorially, patted him on the back, and moved on to talk to another group.

"Interesting stuff," Tom said. "What did you think?"

"I'm not sure. I can't see the system that would support something like that. It would have to be huge."

Tom gripped his chin, stroked at a non-existent mustache, and nodded.

"I mean, logistically, it's just hard to imagine, don't you think?"

"Well, yeah, but that's why I love what I do. Technology is evolving faster than ever. It's exciting to be a part of that."

"True," Gordon conceded.

"And as the capacity for computing increases, so do the possible applications. And we are the ones who get to decide what they will be."

Gordon cocked his head and narrowed his eyes, not sure he followed Tom's reasoning.

"We get to take the tech and apply it specifically to our companies and customers. We get to be the ones to apply it to come up with unique solutions to problems. What we do with it, well, that could turn out to be something that flows out to everyone, everywhere."

Now *that* sounded exciting. "Okay, I see where you're going with this."

"But that's not all, my friend." Tom threw an arm over Gordon's shoulder. "If you want to be a CIO, you need to start paying attention to these kinds of things and always think about how they can be solutions for your employer and for their customers."

Gordon thought about this and then considered what Hank had talked about in his presentation. It was as if a switch flipped in his head, one second off, the next, on. What had just a few minutes earlier seemed almost like science fiction now bounced around in his head as possibilities.

* * *

Almost everyone had just filed out of the most argumentative, highly charged work meeting that Gordon had ever been part of. "That went about as well as I expected." Tom pulled discarded papers and file folders into a stack and tapped them together on the conference room table.

"Is that good or bad?" Jack asked.

Gordon still felt a little shell-shocked. What had he expected for one of the first meetings of the new governance committee, though? There were about twice as many projects as the budget would allow. Of course, everyone would be pushing for the ones that would benefit their own department most. It was not unlike the old way IT projects had been submitted and prioritized in his department. The squeaky wheel was always the one to get greased and today's meeting had felt like a Coliseum battle to be the squeakiest wheel. Somehow, Tom had expertly steered everyone's passionate demands toward a solution that was best for the whole company.

"I didn't think you were going to get Leslie to agree," Jack said. "I'm still not sure she's one hundred percent on board."

"She'll get there." Tom seemed confident, but he hadn't been working with Leslie for six years. He didn't understand her modus operandi. She was fiercely loyal to her department, saw rules as mere suggestions, and viewed her ability to skirt them as one of her best features. Yes, she agreed that the company focus should be on upgrading the ERP, but that didn't mean she wouldn't look for loopholes. Gordon had to side with Jack on this point.

"Okay, just a couple more things from me," Tom said, handing a sheet of paper to Jack and then Gordon. "The way we launch is critical," he started. "We can't just let this project flounder. It must move along at the most efficient rate. To do that requires a certain type of organization."

Gordon nodded and pulled out a pen to take notes.

"The first step in successful project implementation is an IT governance committee that sets priorities and provides resources for the project, and we can check that off our list."

If that meeting was what Tom considered successful, Gordon would need to adjust his expectations.

"Beyond that, we need to have a project steering team that will make sure the ERP upgrade is going smoothly and deadlines are being met. They'll report to the governance committee."

Gordon wrote a few things on his paper, then asked, "Who will be on this team?"

"Someone from the executive team should sponsor it. In this case, it makes sense for that person to be me since the ERP upgrade is a company-wide project. But you will also be part of the team, as IT manager. In fact, I think you should be the project manager."

Gordon narrowed his eyes and tipped his head to the side slightly, as if unsure he'd heard Tom correctly. "Surely they've told you about the last project I tried to manage." Gordon shot Jack a look, but he stayed silent and let Tom do the talking.

"The reason that project failed was because you didn't have this kind of organization." Tom tapped the sheet in front of him. "Before, you didn't have guidelines or methods to manage projects and the results were always mixed. It wasn't just you, either. Many of the projects undertaken in the last few years, even the ones that were considered successful, have failed to deliver the full possible value to Mama Meg's. It's been hit and miss. That's not how we're going to do it this time."

Gordon nodded. "Okay, I'm in."

"Great. We will also need managers who have a stake in this project on the team as well. Jack?" Tom was on a roll. "Will you get Walt, Marcia, Leslie, and Chris to dedicate a department manager to this team?"

Jack nodded and pulled out his phone to take care of it right then.

Turning back to Gordon, Tom continued. "They'll help us gain cooperation from each of the departments so the roll-out can happen efficiently. Together we'll set the direction for the project, make sure that resources are allocated correctly, all while monitoring the progress and the budget."

"Okay, what about the project implementation team?" Gordon asked, pointing to the last heading on Tom's list.

"You'll lead that team, which will be made of people from IT, as well as the subject matter experts from each department. This is where stuff gets done. You'll be on the front lines, getting the functional requirements and taking recommendations from the vendor. You'll be responsible for seeing that testing is done and for making sure the system works as it should. There will need to be post-project review and you and the implementation team will also be responsible for that."

When Tom broke it down into those steps, this huge project seemed doable.

"What we're doing is managing change," Tom said. "All that pushback from our first governance meeting? Totally normal. Change is hard, even if everyone agrees it needs to happen."

"That makes perfect sense," Gordon said. "So essentially, we anticipate problems, try and mitigate them, and communicate?"

"I like that." Jack nodded, and for the first time since the governance meeting, he smiled.

"You got it. All of that, plus manage the ERP update implementation. Should be a cinch." Tom winked.

"And mind the timeline!" Jack quickly added. "Only the whole future of the company depends on it."

Oh, right, Gordon thought. Jack's siblings, Brigitte and Scott, had convinced the board that they should sell Mama Meg's to their biggest competitor, Oven Love, and Jack had one year to change their minds.

So, there was that.

* * *

The weeks raced by in a blur; Gordon hardly noticed the passage of time, only that he never seemed to have enough of it. Making sure everything went smoothly for the ERP implementation was an incredible amount of work. At times he felt like a juggler who kept getting thrown extra balls to keep in the air. But unlike his pre-Tom work life, when he could barely get out of the office before nine, organizing and prioritizing the project meant that everything was given the right amount of attention at the right time. He was busy, yes, but not constantly frantic. Because of this, he was able to leave every day at a reasonable hour, which Tricia very much appreciated. If Gordon remembered correctly, her exact words had been, "Tell Tom he's a genius."

He typed out his weekly status report. Phase one, planning and organization, had been completed. Phase two, configuration and modeling, was also complete. Phase three, testing, was underway. He still had to manage the training, double check his go-live plan, and then finally go live. Gordon felt a surge of pride. He'd hit every timeline goal—which with so many moving parts was no easy task—and Jack was thrilled.

A knock sounded on his door frame, and he looked up to see Walt. In the month and a half that Tom had been there, Gordon had seen his old boss less and less and missed working with him. He had to admit, though, that Tom was a far better mentor, especially now that Gordon was clearer about his career goals.

"Hey, Walt," Gordon said. "What's up?" Walt had been plenty busy with his own work in Finance and didn't make his way down to Gordon's part of the building often.

"I'm guessing you haven't heard the news?" he said, taking a seat in the one chair that wasn't piled high with reams of computer printouts.

Walt had never been much of a gossip, so his apparent eagerness to share some detail of workplace drama caught Gordon off guard. "Uh, I'm not sure. What is it?"

"Leslie just bought her own sales module for the ERP. She went against the recommendations of the governance committee and way over budget. I'm not sure what kind of research she even did, or if it's compatible with our system…" Walt trailed off, seeming more interested in Gordon's reaction than in doling out more information.

All the metaphorical balls Gordon had been juggling started to drop, one by one. What did this mean for the project? How many people would it take from his staff to figure out how to implement it into their current ERP, if that was even possible?

What was this going to do to their timeline? He dropped his head into his hands and groaned.

"I knew something like this was going to happen," Walt said. "I told Jack that this wasn't a good time to make massive changes, that we could come up with other options to scale the business that weren't so pricey."

"Does Tom know?" Gordon asked.

"I think I heard him talking with Jack in his office. Jack is not happy."

Gordon could only imagine. He'd known Leslie was a wild card, but after four weeks, he thought she'd have understood the priorities and gotten on board with the committee's plans. Gordon glanced up at Walt, who had his lips pressed together, like he was repressing a facial expression he didn't want seen. Walt fidgeted, his hands alternating between clasping and wringing in his lap.

"I'm going to suggest we delay the implementation until we can reassess the situation," Walt said, and Gordon thought he caught a tone of gloating in his voice. But that couldn't be right. Why would Walt be happy about this development?

"Gordon, do you have a minute?" Tom said as he entered the office and seemed to read the expressions on the men's faces, assessing the situation. "Hello, Walt. I take it you've shared the latest news about Leslie's purchase?" "Just filling Gordon in. I'd guess you two have some decisions to make. I was just telling him, though, that I'm going to recommend Jack pause implementation." Walt stood up and squared his shoulders, like he was ready for battle.

"Jack's talking with Leslie right now, but I'm sure you can catch him after that," Tom said.

"Good to know." Walt excused himself from Gordon's office and Gordon had to set aside the slightly disturbing realization that his old boss wasn't as upset with this development as he should be. He and Tom had work to focus on and Gordon had a lot of balls to get back into the air.

"Do you think Jack will take Walt's advice and pause implementation? We've got momentum and would lose so much progress if we stopped now."

"Not a chance," Tom said. "Jack is fully committed. Stopping now would be disastrous."

"Walt sure seems interested in stopping it, though. Do you think it's just a budget issue?"

Tom let out a long breath and shook his head. "I don't know. There's something Walt's not telling us, that's for sure. But right now, we've got to fix this mess Leslie made. Good news first." He sat in the chair recently vacated by Walt and Gordon took note that while his voice conveyed the urgency of the situation, Tom's demeanor was under control. "The sales system Leslie picked will integrate with our ERP, so all we have to do is implement that integration. And it's a good program. It will allow sales to operate much more efficiently."

"Okay," Gordon said, trying to square what Tom was saying with Walt's gloom and doom predictions. This didn't sound so bad.

Tom continued. "Bad news—it's probably going to set us back about two weeks. Not the end of the world, but not great either as we're already five months into Jack's one year timeline to turn things around." Tom sighed again. "But there's nothing we can do about that now. We've got to move forward."

"I can pull Shonda and Max off their project and shuffle around a few others to fill in gaps. I'll get them working on the sales module immediately," Gordon said.

"Good."

Gordon couldn't believe Leslie was going to get away with going behind everyone's backs and wondered how much this loss of trust from the rest of the governance and steering committees would affect their progress. "What are you going to do about Leslie?" he asked.

"Jack will deal with it. We will focus on keeping our momentum."

* * *

By July, their persistence and drive paid off, even though the first two weeks of the new ERP system were not without challenges. Gordon and his team had kept busy fixing a handful of vendor configurations and a couple dozen incorrect sku's. They'd pushed so hard and so fast to bring the new system on line that little bugs were to be expected.

Because of the success of the project implementation team, everyone worked together to solve the problems. Since each department had subject matter experts who had attended all the implementation meetings, they had communicated effectively about what was happening, the timeline, and what to do when problems arose. They almost acted like cheerleaders for the project, so that when things went wrong, instead of a loss of morale, or a dusting off of hands, they were able to come together and apply fixes to get things working as they should.

Because of them, everyone company-wide was on the same page and had the same goals. Success was practically guaranteed.

Executives from every department filtered into the conference room. Trays of Mama Meg's cookies sat at intervals down the length of the table.

"Mmm. These are good. Are they new?" Tom asked as he took several more and placed them on the cocktail napkin in front of him.

"Those are from our new organic line," Chris said.

"Marketing is almost ready to roll out the campaign," Marcia added, taking several for herself.

"There's a market for organics?" Gordon asked as Leslie arrived.

"Is there ever!" Leslie said, and Gordon wondered if she'd been standing outside, just waiting for someone to say the perfect thing for her to make her entrance. All eyes landed on her. "I have an announcement. I just finished telling Jack the good news. We've landed the Burger Shack account. Mama Meg's organic cookies will be in every kids' meal for the next nine months. And if that goes well, they'll extend."

"That's huge," Chris said.

"Once kids get a taste and parents see how good they are, we can expect sales to go up in our retail outlets as well," Leslie added. "The potential is huge."

Chris shook his head. "Good thing the ERP is up and running. There's no way we'd be able to coordinate all of this extra work without it."

Kshipra, from purchasing, jumped in. "Since we've been using the updated ERP, it's so much easier to know exactly what we've got in inventory, to look at trends, and make projections. It's like all the information is right there at my fingertips."

For a second, Gordon wondered why Kshipra was there instead of Walt, but lost interest in pursuing that train of thought when Leslie spoke again.

"I know you all were mad when I went rogue and got that sales module, but without it, this sale would have taken a lot longer to close. Oven Love could have swooped in and won the account. So, while I do recognize how wrong I was," Leslie shrugged and grinned, "I think we can all agree it worked out in the end."

Chris wadded up a napkin and threw it at her while at least two others rolled their eyes.

Leslie took the good-natured abuse in stride. "I promise," she held up her hands, palms out, "I'll abide by whatever this committee decides about projects going forward, even if I don't agree."

From the whispered sarcastic comments, it was clear to Gordon that these people would believe it when they saw it. But for now, it appeared Leslie was forgiven. She reached forward and grabbed a few cookies. "They're good, right? They practically sell themselves. Once Burger Shack tasted them the sale was basically mine."

The mood was light as they waited for Jack to arrive so they could start the meeting. It was clear to see that everyone felt a little ownership of this win. They'd all worked to make sure the ERP rollout was a success, and this sale was a direct result of their hard work.

"Has anyone seen Walt?" Jack had rushed into the room, panic in his voice.

The mood of the room chilled instantly. "Not since yesterday morning," Marcia said. "Why?"

Kshipra spoke up. "He left just before noon. He said he felt sick and was going home to rest."

Jack exhaled pure frustration which only added to the sudden tension.

"What's going on, Jack?" Leslie asked.

Jack kneaded his temples, his eyes squeezed into tight, worried lines. The silence stretched out, along with a growing feeling of discomfort. Finally, he spoke. "What I'm about to tell you doesn't leave this room, understand? I just need some time before I made a public statement. *If* I have to make statement. It's possible there's an explanation..."

"Explanation for what?" Chris asked.

"It appears," Jack said, "That Walt's been misrepresenting Mama Meg's financials."

Gordon felt sick and thought back to how cagey Walt had been about Tom, the updated ERP, the whole project in general. Change was hard for everyone, but Walt had been particularly resistant. Was this why? What had his old friend done?

It felt like all the air had gone out of the room. No one spoke. Jack broke the silence.

"All I know is, there's a lot of money missing, and all evidence points to Walt."

Chapter 7

"He did what now?" Leslie put her BlackBerry in the pocket of her blazer and, along with Chris, Gordon, Marcia, and Kshipra, gathered around Laura's glass top desk. The group ignored the white leather chairs with gold accents, instead crowding close enough to Laura's desk that she could have could have whispered and still be heard. She didn't whisper.

"Walt changed the depreciation schedule for the assets," she said, rubbing the edges of her eyes, careful not to smear her makeup. "It happened years ago—so we could secure a loan from the bank." Laura let out a long sigh, her shoulders slumped in near defeat. "He says he tried to fix it many times over the years, but there was never a good time. Mama Meg's had to maintain a certain level of assets for the bank to keep the line of credit open, so he kept fudging the numbers. And it snowballed."

"Good God," Leslie said, her eyes wide with astonishment.

Walt had always been so careful and dependable. He'd seemed, to Gordon, like a paragon of integrity. Gordon never would have guessed he would have done something like this.

"It all makes sense now," Chris said. "That must be why he pushed back on the ERP upgrade, pretty much at every step of the way. He knew what we'd find once we all had access to the data."

In hindsight, it did seem obvious, and Gordon wondered how he'd ignored all the signs.

"Walt has resigned, obviously," Laura added and most everyone responded with solemn nods. Laura sighed before continuing. "This whole thing has caused a bit of a financial catastrophe. Jack's looking for some additional funding, but I would be lying if I said we weren't in a precarious position."

The gravity of the situation settled over Gordon like a lead blanket, a weight on his chest that made it difficult to breathe.

"What if he doesn't get it?" Kshipra asked. "What will happen to Mama Meg's?"

"He'll get it," Laura said, but it was easy to see she was trying to convince herself, as much as everyone else, that this was the case. "In the meantime, let's not lose our momentum. The ERP has got us working at peak efficiency. We can't lose that."

"Agreed," Chris said, and that made sense, because production had never run at such high capacity. They were turning out more product that ever and it was all thanks to the ERP. "Actually," he turned to Gordon, "I could use your help when we're done here."

"Of course," Gordon said, and Laura indicated she was pretty much done with what she had to tell them. They all filed out of her office except for Kshipra, whom Laura asked to stay so they could talk about her filling in until a replacement for Walt could be found.

"What do you need?" Gordon asked, once they were in the hall.

"We're nearly at full production capacity," Chris said. "We've got plans for a new facility, but I'm sure that's going to be on hold for now, until Jack gets funding. Is there anything you can do to do help increase efficiency while we wait for expansion?"

Gordon nodded. "Yeah. I can tweak the supervisory control and data acquisition system (SCADA) to give you a little more info on what's running through lines and where the bottlenecks are. If you can clear some of the bottlenecks, a small SCADA adjustment will help tide you over for a while."

"Perfect. Thanks." Chris held out his fist for a bump and Gordon obliged. "Pretty weird about Walt. Did you see that coming?"

That was what was bugging him so much about this whole thing. He hadn't, and it made him question what else he might be missing. He told Chris as much before they arranged a time for the SCADA update and went their separate ways. Luckily, he was busy enough that he didn't have time to dwell on what Walt had done, so he got back to work and, like Laura had suggested, moved forward.

* * *

The tension at Mama Meg's had simmered for a full week and it was clear that everyone's happy veneer was just one scratch away from revealing their anxiety-ridden interiors. When he showed up at the governance meeting, Gordon could tell the team was done maintaining the charade. They'd all spent the last week keeping up appearances: Leslie had made sales, production had continued to make more product than ever, and Gordon had managed a handful of minor IT projects.

"Have you heard anything?" Chris asked Leslie, who could normally be counted on to have the inside scoop.

This time, she shrugged. "I haven't even heard if Jack got the funding," Leslie admitted. "Kshipra? Do you know?"

She shook her head.

"We don't even know who he's working with, do we?" Gordon asked and got shrugs and confused looks in response.

"I'm afraid to ask," Marcia admitted, and that pretty much summed up the entire last week—no information and a lot of walking on eggshells.

They didn't have time to speculate because at that moment, Laura and Jack arrived at the meeting and a hush fell over the conference room. At first, Jack focused on getting settled, pulling a pen from his shirt pocket and setting his BlackBerry on the table in front of him. When he finally looked up at his executive team, his expression turned grave. "My God. You all look like you're at a funeral," he said dismissively, considering the level of concern they'd all been holding on to.

Gordon looked from Marcia to Chris and could tell they had the same question on the tips of their tongues. In the end, it was Leslie who spoke up. "Well? Is it a funeral, Jack? What the hell is going on with the company?"

Jack paused for a moment before the corner of his mouth quirked, and his eyes brightened. "We got the funding."

The room filled with a collective exhale, and Gordon felt relief fill his whole body.

"Obviously there will be a few organizational changes," Jack said over a thrum of excited chatter, "but for the most part, it's full steam ahead." He briefly outlined the timeline for acquisition of the new manufacturing facility and fielded questions from Chris. Gordon jotted down a list of possible projects that would need consideration by the steering committee in several months when the sale went through, and Jack must have noticed because he unbuttoned the cuffs of his light blue button-down, pushed up his sleeves, and changed track. "Let's get down to the business of governance," he said. "We could sit around, congratulating ourselves on the success of the ERP upgrade, but I think what we should really do is keep this momentum—use the tools and techniques that Tom taught us and do it again."

"I fully agree," Gordon said. "In fact, I was hoping we could come up with ideas for what IT could focus on next. Shall I make a list?" He uncapped the dry erase marker and stepped up to the whiteboard.

He started by listings the items he'd come up with that they'd need to focus on for the new facility. Soon, others were calling out the projects they thought should get attention.

"I think we ought to fix the EDI and make it work this time," Leslie said. "It's critical to both customers and suppliers." She tapped her pen on the yellow pad of paper in front of her. "We can probably make a success of it now."

"I like that idea," Marcia said. "With the new ERP we've got more flexibility with how we handle the EDI configuration."

Gordon made a few quick calculations in his head. "That would take three to four months. I think we have the time before the new facility opens. Jack?"

Jack gave a thumbs up and the suggestions continued.

"We need to get information out of the production line," Chris said. "If we could automate the recipes so that we know exactly what is going in each and every item, so we can calculate ahead of time what our output will be, we could tie that into quality control."

"I like that suggestion too," Leslie said.

"That's a pretty good list," Jack said. "Let's vote."

Gordon couldn't help but recall their first meetings with Tom and how much arguing there had been by everyone trying to get their project to the top of the list. But now, while there had definitely been impassioned comments about the pros and cons of each project, the group seemed to trust the process more. They knew that whatever they chose was going to benefit all of them.

"Looks like we're in agreement," Jack said. "Let's get the EDI module working better. We'll send it to the steering committee and from there, they can identify the subject matter experts. Gordon, can you get a meeting schedule out to everyone by the end of the week?

Gordon nodded and noticed the general mood of excitement over the proposed project. He even heard a couple comments about how much nicer it would be to be able to utilize the EDI. Gordon would be lying if he said he didn't still feel a twinge of guilt about the botched project, but he knew why it had failed the first time and this time would be different.

"Gordon," Jack said when the meeting was over. "Can you stick around for a moment?"

"Sure." He was eager to get back to his desk to start organizing the new EDI project, but he had a few minutes for Jack. He imagined he'd been through a lot in the last week with Walt's resignation and having to secure funding. Chris had told him he'd heard from Laura that things had been pretty dire. After the last person left, Jack shut the door and turned to Gordon.

"With Walt gone and Tom pretty much finished with his contract," Jack started, "that leaves you without a direct manager."

Gordon had thought about this. A lot, actually. Tom was still popping in once or twice a week, but for the most part, he was ready to move on to his next client. Gordon assumed whomever they hired to take Walt's place would probably be his new boss. Whether that was Kshipra or someone else, he figured he would know once the hire was announced.

"These last six months have been challenging. I know we required a lot of you and your team and to be honest, I was impressed with the way you stepped up. You've got a good relationship with the executive team because of your work on the steering committee." Jack ticked the list off on his fingers. "You're comfortable leading, and you've got good internal working relationships within Mama Megs. I've had several discussions with Tom about you and he thinks, and I tend to agree, that you are ready for a director level role."

The suggestion caught Gordon off guard. The IT director role had been on his radar and was an important step toward becoming a CIO, but he hadn't thought the promotion would happen so soon.

Jack continued. "One thing I've learned over the last few months with Tom, and with Emmett before him, is just how crucially important IT is to Mama Meg's success."

"I totally agree," Gordon said.

"So if you want the new role, you'd need to step in and take control of some of the things Tom was working on. You'll lead the steering committee. And you'll report directly to me. How does that sound?"

Gordon had a few questions for Jack before he accepted, but knew this was the direction he'd wanted his career to go. It was an easy choice.

"Absolutely," Gordon said. "I accept." He immediately imagined what Tricia would say when he walked in the door with this news. He thought of Jacob and little Hannah, just starting to crawl. As soon as he got back to his office, he'd call his wife and tell her to pick a restaurant for dinner so they could go out and celebrate tonight.

* * *

Gordon pulled into the parking lot behind McMenamins Pub, grabbed his book, and made his way inside the building. Six months as IT director for Mama Megs had been exhilarating and he'd risen to the challenge in every way. The second attempt at the EDI project had been a huge success. Chris, Kshipra, and even Leslie had sung its praises daily for weeks after the project wrapped.

From there he'd managed the technical aspect of the manufacturing expansion, bringing operations online and combining the two facilities' SCADA systems information into the materials requirement planning software. Max and Shandra had both been promoted to IT managers, Max at the original Mama Meg's facility and Shandra at the new location. He'd run the steering committee and together they'd prioritized projects and, amazingly, kept everyone happy.

But recently, things had started to feel stale. He'd worked for Mama Meg's for eight years and helped them grow from a strong regional brand to an emerging national brand. Now everything felt like it was on auto pilot. Systems were in place, things were running fairly smoothly, and his team was competent and hardworking. Tricia was glad he was home by five-thirty nearly every day, but Gordon missed the excitement that came with challenging himself.

"Hey, Gordon," Tom said from the bar. "Everyone's in the back room. What did you think of the book?"

He held up his copy of *Computer Confluence*. They were lucky to get the author to join them for tonight's book club and Gordon had been looking forward to this SIM meeting all day. "Fascinating," he replied. "Can't wait to discuss it."

Gordon ordered a burger, tater tots, and one of the pub's craft ales and went back to grab a seat.

"Hey, Gordon," several of his SIM friends called, waving him over to an open spot at their table. They chatted while he waited for his food, the conversation changing from work to the Portland Beavers, the town's minor league baseball team, then back to work and IT.

Paul said, "All of our sales people just got new Blackberries and we have to figure out a way to manage those myriad devices from a single web-based control room. This RIM platform is great, though, because we'll be able to remotely enable access to email and contacts, manage lost hardware, establish security policies, and push notifications."

"Push notifications?" Gordon's friend Howard said. "That could be fun." They all laughed.

"Yeah, but what do you think about the tech?" Gordon asked between bites. "Do you think it has staying power? I hear Apple's developing their own operating system."

Dina, a woman Gordon had only met a couple times, exhaled sharply. "Apple is famous for using the exclusivity of their product to shut large swaths of people out of the market. I don't think we'll have anything to worry about."

Another man piped up. "I don't know. Have you seen the new iPod? That's a good-looking product and I heard it can hold over two hundred songs."

Their conversation was interrupted by the president of their SIM chapter introducing the speaker, a technology researcher based in Silicon Valley. And while the presentation was interesting, Gordon's mind was elsewhere. He couldn't predict exactly what was going to happen with the phone technology, but something in the back of his mind told him he needed to be paying more attention to other platforms. BlackBerry was the industry standard for business smart phones, but that didn't mean they'd be on top forever. When you were on top, it was too easy to relax and get comfortable and stop looking for better and different ways to do things. It was so easy to go through the motions; to get lazy.

The thought struck him. *He* was a BlackBerry. Right now, at Mama Meg's, he was effective and excellent at what he did, but there was no need to change or challenge himself. He could easily see himself getting more comfortable and slipping into irrelevance. Gordon squirmed in his seat. The speaker's words washed over him, and he only had the slightest notion of what was being said. In his head, he updated his resume and imagined a new life without his Mama Meg's work family; he felt both conflicted and excited about a possible change.

The speaker took questions and the audience seemed engaged. Vaguely aware that Tom was asking a question, Gordon took out a pen and started to make notes on his napkin. Not about the speaker, but about ideas for people to connect with and companies to reach out to. He'd need to think about posting his resume on Monster.

"Well, that was interesting, wasn't it?" Howard said. "You certainly took a lot of notes."

"Huh?" Gordon looked up and was surprised to see that the talk was over, and people had gotten up and were milling around. "Oh, this?" He held up the napkin before tucking it into his shirt pocket. "Actually, I was making some notes about something else. I think it's time for me to look for a new job."

"Really," Howard said. "Remind me what you do again?"

Gordon filled him in on everything he'd been doing as IT director while his friend nodded intently.

"You know," Howard looked thoughtful, "there's a job open for IT director at MedConnect. I know someone who works there, and I'd be happy to give them your resume. It's manufacturing, but it's manufacturing of medical devices. It would be a big change from cookies, that's for sure."

"It sounds promising," Gordon said. "I'd be interested in learning more."

The man tapped his BlackBerry a few times. "I'm sending you my contact info now. Why don't you reach out to me on Monday?"

"Perfect," Gordon said. "And thank you."

Chapter 8
June 2005

The lobby of MedTech was a soaring, two-story, glass and stainless-steel wonder that would have been too bright if not for the fifteen-foot living wall of plants. The air was cool and fresh and didn't smell one bit like cookies. The contrast between the sleek and modern design elements with the organic greenery felt like a nod to the work this company did combining cutting edge technology with lifesaving machines. It was difficult not to feel the importance of that just sitting in the lobby.

"Gordon, good morning and welcome." Gordon's new boss, Colin Bateman, COO of MedTech, approached with an outstretched hand. "Ready for your first day?"

"Absolutely." Gordon shook Colin's hand enthusiastically. "I'm excited to get started." He followed alongside Colin after the man gestured that they should walk and talk.

"As I mentioned in our interviews, the IT department is in desperate need of some leadership, so I know that many people will be just as excited that you're here."

Gordon picked up on what Colin left unspoken. Many were excited he was here, but some were not. He added that to his list of things to work on and followed as Colin used his key card to get them back into the office space.

"I thought I could show you around this morning, introduce you to a few of the people you'll need to know. Then we can swing by HR and get your badge taken care of."

"Sounds good," Gordon said as they entered a wide-open space filled with low-walled cubicles. Windows covered the south wall, letting in light and exposing a park-like setting just outside. Azaleas and rhododendrons in pinks, purples, and oranges dotted the landscaping with beautiful greenery interspersed. Benches and trickling fountains seemed to be placed strategically for optimum viewing of nature. What this place would lack in free cookies, it certainly made up for with its calming aesthetics.

"This is sales and marketing," Colin swept his arm out, indicating the cubicles, "but I thought we could start with the Engineering Department."

Gordon figured Engineering would rely quite a bit on IT, so he knew he needed to make a strong connection with the manager. "I've read up about the equipment you design. There seems to be a lot of technology in every device."

"It's an exciting time to be part of the medical field with so much innovation happening. Take our blood pressure cuffs and thermometers, for example. The information they gather from patients updates directly to that patient's chart. It saves nurses time for having to hand write everything, and it eliminates mistakes in both the recording and reading of the information. Nurses and doctors then use the data our machines collect to look at and track trends. That way, the data can work harder, and medical professionals can have more information to make better decisions." Colin led Gordon down a hallway and into another part of the building. He opened a door and held it while Gordon passed through.

"That sounds like exciting work."

"It is. We're not so much a medical equipment manufacturing company as much as we are a medical information gathering company." Colin knocked on an office's door frame. "Here's Clete Winston, our engineering manager." He poked his head in, then motioned for Gordon to follow. "Clete, this is Gordon Rusbart, the new IT Director."

"Hello." Clete's face barely registered emotion with the greeting, and he made no move to extend his hand. "You've got your work cut out for you." Clete pushed back in his chair and stretched out. "These days the IT department is either too slow or completely useless."

Gordon returned to his mental list and moved *Win over Clete Winston* to the top. "I'm sorry to hear that," Gordon said. "What do you think the problem is?" The engineering department could be IT's biggest problem, but they probably held the key to solving IT's problems. At least some of them. Gordon knew a little diplomacy and patience would go a long way with Clete.

"I have no idea. I don't have time to figure it out. We're busy creating life-saving equipment. All I know is that whenever we have a problem, we call IT only as a last resort."

"Now, Clete," Colin said. "This is Gordon's first day. Maybe save your complaining for his second week." Colin chuckled at his joke, but Clete's expression didn't change.

"I don't know exactly what's going on over there, but you can be assured I'm going to look into it and changes will be coming. I just ask that you give me a chance," Gordon said.

Clete shrugged. "Expectations are low, so I guess you've got that working for you."

They chatted for a minute longer. It was painfully clear to Gordon that Clete wasn't a fan of small talk, so he was glad when they finally moved on. "Don't worry too much about him," Colin said as they headed toward the finance department. "You know how engineers can get."

Gordon didn't. He hadn't really worked with engineers before, but if the rest of them were anything like Clete, winning them over with charm was not going to work. He'd need results.

Compared to Engineering, Finance was a delight. He met the finance manager and several others who had valuable feedback about their experience with IT. While they had complaints similar to Clete's, they seemed a little more understanding. To come up with solutions to fix IT, getting feedback, no matter how negative, was crucial.

"This is HR," Colin said as they walked into another area, then greeted the receptionist. "Hi, Lucy. Is Linda in?"

A tall, impeccably dressed woman appeared from one of the offices. "Is this our new hire?" she said, before Lucy even had time to reply. She made her way toward Colin and Gordon, her hand outstretched. "Welcome to MedTech." Gordon took her hand. "I got a peek at your resume, and I have to admit being a little jealous that you got to spend so many years at a cookie company. It sounds like a pretty great place to work. All those cookies!"

Gordon answered Linda's questions, amused with this woman's show of delight.

"This conversation is making me hungry for cookies," she said. "I'm going to have to pick up some Mama Meg's Monkey Nutters on the way home. Those are my favorite." She promised to bring Lucy some, then turned back to Gordon. "Let's get you your badge," she said, instructing him to sit in a chair against a blue backdrop. She took several pictures and let him pick his favorite. "If you want to wait around, I should have it for you in about ten minutes. Otherwise, I can drop it off at your new office a little later."

"Why don't you drop it off," Colin said, guiding Gordon out of HR with his hand on his shoulder. "We still have a few people I want Gordon to meet." They headed back toward sales and marketing. "I guess I know where to stop by tomorrow for a cookie," Colin mused.

Gordon laughed. He'd had so many cookies in the years he worked for Mama Meg's, he figured it would be a while before they excited him again. What was exciting to him now was turning MedTech's IT department around. After quick introductions to the sales director and the marketing director, they finally made it to the IT department.

"Let me show you to your new office," Colin said, and he ushered Gordon into a space that was twice as big as his office at Mama Meg's. Light streamed in from the windows—he had windows!—and Gordon could just see the plants and trees in the natural area in the courtyard below. His office furniture matched the style of décor he'd seen in the lobby and there was even a green plant on his desk with a little notecard that read *Welcome to MedTech,* signed by Linda and "the HR team."

"William," Colin said. "Come in. I want you to meet Gordon."

Gordon turned to see a short man in a blue shirt and red striped tie, his dark hair slicked into a side part.

"Nice to meet you." William extended his hand and shook Gordon's vigorously. "So glad you're here. I look forward to working together." There was a buzz and he pulled a pager from the holder at his waist and read the message. A hiss leaked from his lips, clearly a curse that he changed into a benign noise at the last minute. "Sorry." He returned his attention to Gordon. "This thing goes off all the time."

"Is that something you need to deal with?" Gordon asked.

"No, no. It's fine," he started to say, but then got distracted by someone walking past Gordon's office. "Hey, Claire." The woman stopped and backed up. "Go get Javier and Duane and come back to meet our new director."

Claire ran back from the way she'd just come while William's pager went off another time. While he checked it, Colin got ready to leave.

"There should be a company directory on your desk next to the phone. If you need anything, just give me a call," Colin said. "But I think I'll let William introduce you to the team and you can get started."

Gordon thanked him and turned his attention to the woman and two men who squeezed into his office as Colin made his exit. Gordon invited them to sit on the black leather couch and pulled two chairs over so he and William could sit down as well.

"Gordon," William said, "this is Claire. She's in charge of the help desk."

Gordon nodded in greeting to the young woman in black pants, a black cardigan, and a black t-shirt. She had a small silver stud in her nose.

William continued. "Javier is our infrastructure manager."

Gordon greeted the brown-eyed man who wore pants that looked a couple inches too short for his generous height.

"And this is Duane, our applications manager."

Duane wore a short sleeve, button-down shirt in reds and greens with a yellow t-shirt underneath. "Nice to meet you," Gordon said.

There was a beep and all three of them checked pagers attached at their waists.

"Mine," Claire said as she pulled it out of the holder and read the message.

"Sorry we're so distracted," William said. "Things are crazy here."

"I can see that," Gordon said, with a small smile. "What kinds of help desk tickets are you responding to?"

"Mostly computer problems and basic networking stuff," Claire said. "We're pretty much a break-fix operation at this point."

"IT is getting dragged into all kinds of stuff we shouldn't be doing," William said. "Engineering is kicking our butts," Duane added. "We don't have the knowledge or tools to diagnose and fix their specialized software. IT doesn't even know what it does, and yet they call us for fixes on it all the time and get upset when we don't deliver."

Javier jumped in. "Those guys are smart. They can do crazy math and figure out how to make machines do amazing things, but they don't know anything about their software. The only way the helpdesk can help is to refer the ticket to vendor support." Javier's pager beeped and he grabbed it, read the message, and answered with his thumbs.

"Do all the helpdesk calls come in on your pagers?" Gordon asked. "That doesn't seem like the most efficient set up."

"The calls come into the helpdesk and if they can't solve the problem, they page one of us," Claire said.

"We've tried to change the process and make things more streamlined, but every time we make one change, it seems to upset the whole system," William said. "It's like every problem is a fire and people want theirs put out first."

"Okay." Gordon dipped his head, giving himself a second to organize his thoughts. He knew that the most important thing was to focus on gaining trust and support internally. He remembered Tom teaching him about the IT pyramid. No pyramid could ever stand without a strong base. So that's where they'd start. At the base. He needed to gain the confidence and trust of everyone at MedTech. "The first thing we should do is a satisfaction survey."

Claire's eyes widened into a look of terror.

"I don't know if that's the best idea," William said.

"Why not?" Gordon had a feeling he knew the answer, but he wanted to hear them say it.

"First of all, it will take time and we don't have time," Javier pointed out.

"Right, and we already know how people feel about our services. They don't like them. Why not spend time trying to make things better rather than asking people to tell us we stink?" Duane added.

"If we want to know what needs fixing, we need to get specific feedback," Gordon said, and tried to hide his amusement when he saw how uncomfortable the thought seemed to make everyone.

"I guess we can do that," William said. "But it's going to be painful."

Gordon smiled warmly. "Trust me. It's critical to know where we are and have a clear starting point. We can't measure improvement otherwise. It might be hard to hear where we're failing, but it will be for the best in the long run."

"That makes sense." Javier hesitated even as he admitted it.

Gordon continued. "After that, I'm going to put together the service catalog and bring in ITIL guidelines."

"ITIL? What's that?" Duane asked.

"It's the Information Technology Infrastructure Library and it can help us create a clear menu of services IT will provide, as well as provide direction on how we can best provide those services. When it's clear what we can and can't do, and when we communicate that clearly, we'll have a better foundation for moving forward."

Claire nodded as Gordon laid out the plan, visibly enthusiastic. "Okay, this is making me actually excited for my job instead of ..." When her pager buzzed, she grabbed it reflexively, and shook the little black box for emphasis. " ... instead of dreading it!"

"If you all can stick with me while we make some changes, within a few weeks, you should be able to turn those pagers off for good."

"I'd like to throw mine in the Columbia River," Duane said under his breath.

"You won't have to go that far." Gordon said. "I'll train you on ITIL and then we can focus on the service management portion of ITIL for the first step in this process."

Later that week, the satisfaction surveys came trickling in. Clete's was among the first and as Gordon had suspected, he had some pretty strong opinions. Gordon had to admire the engineering manager's commitment to thoroughly answering some of the write-in questions, often giving novel-length answers that went onto the back of the page. After compiling the data from all the surveys, it became clear that the problems with the IT department started with the helpdesk.

Gordon had tasked Claire with putting together a team to categorize all the incident tickets the helpdesk had responded to over the last three years. It was a headache of a task thanks to the lack of organization, but within a few weeks, some clear patterns began to emerge.

Now, sitting in Gordon's office, Claire pushed the sleeves of her chunky black sweater up to her elbows and pulled out her notebook and pen. "We still have a lot of work to do to create the full incident history, but we're seeing a large number of tickets that have to do with helping people change their password." She tapped her notebook with her pen. "This certainly seems like something people should be doing themselves. It's taking up a huge chunk of our time."

"Let's look at coming up with a training element," Gordon suggested.

"What if we made a little sticker that went on every monitor that had the steps for changing passwords?" Claire offered.

"That's a great idea. Will you look into that?" Claire nodded and Gordon turned to Duane. "How's it going categorizing services? This is a crucial first step to creating our services catalog, so we want to make sure to get it right."

"I won't lie," Duane said. "I'm seeing stuff that's miscategorized or not categorized at all. It's a little challenging to even define some of these services we provide."

Gordon nodded. He'd felt the same way when he'd worked on a similar project at Mama Meg's. "Think about services in categories," he said. "For example, think about communications as a category of service. You'd include email and phones as a service within that category. Another category might be called *infrastructure* and would include the servers, the networks, and network equipment."

Duane stroked his chin as he considered everything Gordon was saying. "Okay. This makes sense."

"I agree it's a little painful with records that are as chaotic as ours, but going through the ticket history and creating these categories is crucial to having a solid services catalog."

"This information is so helpful," Duane said, twirling his pen in his fingers, "but I do have just one more problem. There's a chunk of service tickets that we weren't able to resolve. Most of them are from the Engineering department. I'm not sure how to categorize them because we don't have the ability to resolve them."

"Hmm." Gordon nodded. The Engineering department had been most vocal on their satisfaction surveys. Gordon had known he'd have to dig deeper to get to the root of the problem. "Let me take that one," he told Duane. "I'll talk to Clete and follow up in our next meeting. Maybe we can't fix their software when they have problems, but there may still be something we can do to help."

Gordon set up a time to meet with Clete the next day and found no less chilly of a reception than he had on his first day. Clete at least offered him a seat and Gordon took that as a win.

"We're engineers," Clete said when Gordon brought up his dissatisfaction with IT. "We know what we're doing when it comes to computers. That's why we usually try and take a stab at things ourselves before we call IT. Also, it's why we know IT is doing a horrible job."

"You've got specialized software and your set-ups are way more complex than any other computers in the company. Our guys aren't equipped to troubleshoot and resolve your issues when it comes to your software."

"That's obvious," Clete said. "But the way things are set up, right now I've got to put in a request with IT before we can escalate, and it hamstrings us. When our programs are down, our work backs up and productivity takes a nosedive. It's incredibly frustrating."

The problem was, Gordon realized, that the software vendor should be the one handling Engineering's problems, but IT still needed to track every time an issue arose. Right now they weren't always being told when there was a problem. "We've been working on setting up standard responses to every IT incident. This will streamline the process and help problems get solved in a timely manner," Gordon said. "What I'd like to do for you is create a standard response for your software issues so when you contact IT with a software issue, they route you directly to the vendor."

"That still sounds like it's going to take a long time," Clete said, unconvinced.

"Not if we all work together. Your engineers need to reach out to IT as soon as problems arise and not try and fix them themselves. Our helpdesk will have a default protocol they'll follow every time so that the right people are working to fix your problem as quickly as possible."

"In theory, it sounds good," Clete said. "I'm not sure I trust that it will actually happen."

"The way I see it, you can keep doing what you're doing and have the same loss of productivity. Or you can work with us and possibly have a better experience." Gordon shrugged and threw out his palms. "According to you, it can't get worse than what you're dealing with now."

Clete's chin quivered, and the corners of his mouth rose ever so slightly into a smile. Dear God, the man could actually smile!

"Fine," he said. "We'll work with you."

* * *

"I'm running into a lot of resistance with some of our team members," Javier said. "They say this new way of doing things is just creating more work for them."

"Obviously it's more work now, but things were so disorganized," William said. "You have to break a few eggs to make an omelet, as they say."

"We know that," Gordon said. "But have we communicated that to everyone in the department?"

Claire looked at Duane, who looked at Javier and William, then they all looked at Gordon.

"I mean, sort of," Claire said.

"Isn't it obvious what we're doing?" Duane said.

"I think it's obvious," Javier added.

"We can't assume anything," Gordon said. "And part of this whole service catalog roll out will be managing change, not just for our IT department, but for everyone in the company. We're asking them to change how they interact with the helpdesk, and we have the highest chance of success if we can make that change comfortable for everyone."

"Well, what do you suggest?" William asked Gordon.

"We need to do some training. We'll start with IT and then we can come up with some way to communicate with the rest of the company," Gordon said. "This project we're doing has three parts: managing incidents—that is, getting the user up and running as fast as possible with little disruption to their routine or productivity; problem management—where we look at the incidents and notice trends; and change management, in which we try to have as little impact as possible on the surrounding processes and work patterns. We're well into the first two. Now we need to think about the third."

"Every time we've tried to change even one thing, we've had ten other things go wrong." Javier crossed his long leg over his knee and continued. "I think people are worried that we're pulling blocks from a Jenga tower and it's all going to come crashing down. Some people want to just protect the Jenga tower we have, even though it's got lots of holes and is completely unstable."

"That's understandable," Gordon said. "So, let's have some contingencies and communicate them. We can have a plan for backing it out if something gets impacted negatively. Do you think that will ease people's minds?" he asked his team.

They were silent for a moment, and it seemed as though each of them were considering his words carefully.

Finally, Duane spoke. "I hope it does, because this service catalog we're putting together is not just a promise we're making to everyone who works here, it's also a promise to us, in a way."

"Right. We don't have to reinvent the wheel for every new incident that gets called into the helpdesk. It's truly going to make all of our jobs easier," Claire said.

"Now we just need to make sure everyone else understands that," said Javier.

* * *

Gordon appreciated the abundance of windows at the MedTech office building, especially in March, when it had been raining for months. Despite the endless grey days, the building still let in as much light as possible. He settled into the chair behind his desk and pulled up the results of his latest IT satisfaction survey. When he'd first arrived, ten months ago, they'd had a 55% approval rating. Now they were at 75% and that number was trending up. Gordon looked up when he heard a knock on his doorframe and was greeted with the stony, reserved face of Clete Winston.

"Hey Clete. Come on in."

The engineering manager pulled his chair right up to Gordon's desk and placed a brown paper sack on the desktop. "Turkey cranberry panini with havarti," he said, pulling a wrapped sandwich from the sack. "And a Cubano for me."

"Thanks," Gordon said, pulling his sandwich from the wrapper and taking a bite. He let out a groan. "This is so good."

"You're buying next week," Clete said.

"I know. And I'm sure you won't let me forget it."

Clete laughed. "Listen, I appreciate the feedback your team had on our current software."

Gordon took a drink from his water bottle. "Well, I appreciate you convincing your team to let us be involved, even peripherally, in your software incidents. Even though we can't fix all of them, tracking the trends of your service issues is still good information for us to have."

"I will happily admit that you were right to standardize IT's service. Even if some of the lower priority issues are taking a few days to address, we know that our incident tickets aren't being ignored. That goes a long way toward building confidence."

"Hey, we're at 97% resolution rate," Gordon bragged.

Clete took another bite of his sandwich. "Yeah, you've mentioned that a few times." His friendly scowl held no malice. "You're not going to try and explain the IT pyramid to me again, are you?"

"As long as you don't start talking about your ISO 9001 certification process. I don't have time for a nap today," Gordon said between bites.

Clete rolled his eyes and took another bite of his Cubano. "Actually, your metrics and my ISO 9001 certification are kind of the same thing if you think about it," he said.

"I'd rather not, but I'm sure you're going to tell me," Gordon teased and the corner of Clete's mouth quirked with amusement.

"I'm serious," Clete said. "With ISO 9001 I'm standardizing quality for products and with your metrics and whatever that manual is called …"

"ITIL," Gordon supplied.

"Right. You're standardizing quality for services."

"I suppose you're right," Gordon said.

Chapter 9
April 2007

Seven-year-old Hannah Rusbart stood stock still in the middle of the MedTech lobby, staring up at the kinetic sculpture of birds in flight. White wings flapped gently in the air blowing from the vents. A slow stream of employees flowed around them on either side as they arrived to work.

"Come on, sweetie," Gordon encouraged. "We've got lots of other fun things to see and do today." He took his daughter's hand and guided her past the reception desk, her neck still craned toward the hanging art on the vaulted ceiling.

"When I'm boss of my company," Hannah said, "I'm going to have one of those, too."

"Are you, now?" Gordon said. "I'm sure all of your employees will love seeing it every day when they come to work." Hannah had eagerly anticipated *Bring Your Daughter to Work Day* at MedTech, counting it down with a paper chain she'd torn a link from each day for the last month.

"Welcome," Rose said cheerily, from behind the reception desk. Up until now, Rose had rarely given Gordon more than a curt nod upon his daily arrival. "I have some special things for you," she said, coming around to present Hannah with a branded lanyard and water bottle. "You can fill your bottle at any of the drinking fountains, and when you have lunch, if your dad says it's okay, maybe you can fill it with a little soda."

"Thanks, Rose," Gordon said as Hannah's grip tightened in his hand. "I think today is definitely a soda day. Hannah is very excited," Gordon said. "Aren't you, honey?"

Hannah nodded. "I'm learning how to be a boss at school," she said, seriously.

"Are you now?" Rose adopted Hannah's solemn tone. "What exactly are you learning?"

"Math and computers," she replied. "I get a hundred on all my tests."

Rose looked rightly impressed and Gordon felt a surge of pride. "You better get going, then," Rose said. "They'll be waiting for you in HR."

Gordon slowed his pace so her little legs could keep up as he moved through the now-familiar hallways. A large platter of cookies greeted them at HR and several tables were set up where other employees' daughters were working on word searches while waiting to get their picture taken for their very own badge. Hannah dropped Gordon's hand and went toward the cookies, unable to resist their pull. She turned back to her dad, a question in her eyes. *Can I have one?*

"They're breakfast cookies," Linda said, as if this now made eating cookies at nine in the morning acceptable.

Gordon wondered if Linda had kids and if she knew how they often reacted to sugar. If she didn't, she was about to find out. "Sure, you can have one, Hannah." He helped her place a cookie on a napkin and saw her to a seat at the table. "I'm going to my office now, but you'll probably see me on your tour. And then we can meet for lunch. Sound good?"

Hannah nodded. "Mm-kay," she said through a mouthful of cookie. She barely turned to say goodbye, her attention fully on the word search in front of her.

Okay then. She seemed to be in good hands. Gordon slipped out and made his way to the IT department. William found him almost as soon as he got to his office and sat down at his desk.

"I can't even imagine bringing my daughter to work a couple years ago," William said by way of greeting, sliding onto Gordon's couch. "It would have been a disaster with how chaotic our department was back then. Imagine how many young girls we would have discouraged from STEM careers. It would have been a tragedy."

"Good thing we've got it together now," Gordon said. "I got the numbers yesterday afternoon for last quarter and the helpdesk's response time continues to improve."

"Good. Claire's doing a great job with training and Duane has completed the roll out of the services catalog."

"That's definitely made a difference in our satisfaction rating."

"I don't think we would have been able to navigate the printer fiasco last month as well as we did without a standard response process."

"Agreed." Gordon and his team had consulted in the purchase of several dozen new printers. They'd researched to ensure that the printers would be compatible with all the desktops, but when the printers were brought online, they learned that many desktops hadn't been updated and didn't have the right software to pair with the printer. It was a hassle, but protocols had been put in place to systematically take care of the issues and get everyone connected as quickly as possible.

Once everything settled down and Gordon had time to reflect, he'd thought about what would happen if something similar happened with their customers and their medical equipment. He'd put the idea off to the side while he focused on other work, but the question bothered him again, now, as he spoke with William. He needed to get more information about how MedTech's products were actually used in clinics and hospitals to ensure a good use experience for their customers.

Around ten-thirty, several HR staffers brought the group of daughters to the IT department as part of their company tour and Gordon sprang into action, meeting them outside of his office.

"This is Gordon. He's the IT director," one of the young staffers explained.

"I already know that," Hannah said proudly. "He's my dad."

The young man looked like he'd momentarily lost his place in his script and Gordon laughed, rushing to the rescue. "That's right. This is the IT department. Do any of you know what we do here in IT?" Gordon scanned the sea of faces. "Anyone besides Hannah?" His daughter dropped her arm and did little to cover a scowl.

When no one volunteered to take a guess, Gordon continued. "We take care of all the systems that help this company run more efficiently." He thought he'd simplified things, but he didn't see the light of understanding in any of the faces.

"We keep the computers running," Claire said from across the office. Gordon could see their interest pique as they looked at the woman in black tights, a black swing dress, and black Doc Martens boots. A purple streak ran through her hair and her ears displayed a small jewelry shop's worth of silver hoops.

Gordon knew when to pass the baton. "Claire, come meet our future businesswomen," he said, waving her over. Gordon slipped away as Claire took over the presentation, doing a much better job with all the young girls, who suddenly had lots of questions.

When he met her at lunch, Hannah had her MedTech lanyard with her badge around her neck, her MedTech water bottle from earlier, and a MedTech stress ball that she clutched possessively. "Can I fill this with soda now?" she said, holding out her bottle, and Gordon led her to the soda fountain.

They made sandwiches from large trays of deli meat and cheese and grabbed chips, fruit, and a cookie to round out their meal. Gordon found them a seat looking out over the garden.

"Are you having fun?" he asked before taking a bite of his sandwich.

"Yeah," Hannah replied through a mouth full of food.

"What's been your favorite part?" he asked, then added, "Besides coming to see me?"

His daughter rolled her eyes and Gordon suppressed a laugh.

"I liked it when we got to try out the blood pressure machine," she said. "And they let us take each other's temperature. I was ninety-seven, which is still normal. I asked."

"Glad to hear it."

"I liked the temperature machine. Can we get one at home?"

"No, that's just for the hospitals and doctor's offices."

"Why?"

"Because it's special. It helps the nurses keep track of a lot of people's temperatures at the same time. We don't need that at home. We just have to keep track of one person's temperature. Maybe two. Besides, it wouldn't work with our computer."

"Why not?"

"It just doesn't."

"That's dumb. What if a doctor doesn't have the right computer? Does he have to go buy a new one from the store?"

Gordon knew Hannah's questions were earnest and struggled to know how to explain to her so she'd understand. But something else pricked his mind as he was thinking of the best way to answer her questions. It was the thing he'd been thinking of since their issue with the incompatible printers. The only way to learn more about the customer needs would be to visit them in person.

The rest of the day passed with Hannah filling out an activity book about MedTech with word puzzles and coloring pages while curled up on the couch in his office, but by three in the afternoon, she started to get antsy. Gordon decided to head home and finish the rest of his work there.

He maneuvered his car home through early afternoon traffic, listening to Hannah's excited chatter. "Can I come back tomorrow?" she asked. Without pausing she added, "Maybe you can put a small desk, just my size, in your office and I can work with you?"

"What about school?" he said. "How will you learn to be a boss if you don't go to class?" While Hannah pondered the question, Gordon had time to think. Tomorrow he would stop by the office of LeeAnne Lamott, the sales manager. If there was a specific way he could use technology to improve patient care, he'd figure it out.

The next morning, Gordon stopped by the sales department first thing. He found LeeAnne, her phone cradled to her shoulder, mid-conversation. She made eye contact and motioned Gordon in, gesturing to a chair.

"Sorry about that," she said after a minute. "Just finishing up some business. What can I do for you?"

Gordon got right to the point. "I think I might have some ideas for how we can help our customers, but I really need to get out there and see for myself what's going on so I can be sure," Gordon said. "Would it be possible for me to go on sales calls?"

LeeAnne gave him an appraising look. Gordon's request had her intrigued. "I like it," she said. "More added value for our customers means they'll keep buying from us. What exactly did you have in mind?" Her phone rang and she waved it off. "Voicemail will get it. Talk to me."

Gordon explained what he'd been thinking while LeeAnne listened patiently. "I want to look at what's going on in the hospitals and clinics. I need to see how our product is getting used so I can understand how it can be improved."

She nodded and looked thoughtful for a moment. "Fatima has accounts with Blessed Heart Hospital, as well as several clinics. She'd be a great person to shadow." LeeAnne pushed up the sleeves of her royal blue blazer, pulled her iPhone toward her, and tapped the screen several times. "I'll text you her number and you can set something up."

Gordon's Nokia vibrated in his belt-holder and he unclipped it. "Got it," he said, seeing LeeAnne's text.

"And keep me updated. If you've got something I can use to give my salespeople an edge, I want to know about it."

"You'll be one of the first to know," Gordon assured her. As soon as he got back to his office, he called Fatima. She seemed as enthusiastic about the idea of Gordon tagging along on her sales calls has LeeAnne had been, and they quickly made plans for him to accompany her in two days.

* * *

"Blessed Heart has been using our products for the last five years," Fatima explained as they made their way from the parking garage to the main hospital building. "We'll swing by and talk with the lab manager, and then the director of nursing. That should help you develop a view of how our products are being used in the real world." She led the way to a bay of elevators, then down a maze of hallways. Clearly, she'd been here before. "Here comes trouble," she said as they approached a man in blue scrubs and red Crocs. "Gordon, this is Matt Scott, the lab manager here at Blessed Heart."

Gordon extended his hand, smiling. "Good to meet you." Matt clasped Gordon's hand with a firm shake.

"Gordon's the director of our IT department and wanted to get an idea of how you're using our products."

"But I also wanted to find out where some of your pain points are," Gordon added. "What do you wish the products did differently? What changes, if any, would make patient care easier?"

Matt brought them both back into the lab while he spoke. "I can't tell you how great it is having integrated technology. It saves me time and has eliminated so many mistakes. I only wish that your machines worked with machines from other manufacturers. If the various pieces of equipment were better integrated, we'd have a consistent view of the patient information available to the nursing staff and doctors."

Gordon nodded, his mind whirring. He'd been hearing about a universal interface called HL-7 for transfer of clinical and administrative data between software applications used by various healthcare providers. This could be a solution to the problem. He'd need to talk with Clete when he returned to MedTech to see about the state of integrating the HL-7 protocol into all of MedTech's equipment.

They chatted some more, then exited through large double doors that swung open when Matt pressed a touch pad in the wall. "You should talk to Kaylee," Matt said. "She's the director of nursing and has opinions on everything."

There was a hint of mischief in Matt's eye and Gordon wondered if he was getting set up. It didn't matter, though, because he needed to know what was working as well as what wasn't. If Kaylee had opinions on that, he needed to know.

They found her in her office, two floors up. Fatima made introductions and Matt excused himself to get back to his work.

Kaylee's face lit up when Fatima explained why they were there. "You want to know what my biggest hassles are?" she said, chuckling to herself. "Pull up a chair. This might take a while."

"That bad, huh?" Gordon asked, taking a seat and raising his eyebrows at Fatima.

She shrugged. "Okay, I may exaggerate a little, but I'll tell you this...a huge chunk of my issues come from inefficient triage, or patients self-presenting." She elaborated when she saw the confusion on Gordon's face. "That's when people come in without an appointment or a recommendation from their general practitioner. It mostly happens in our ER and labor and delivery ward, obviously, but nine times out of ten, that patient could have treated themselves at home."

Gordon thought he understood, but he wanted to be sure. "Why does this cause so many problems?"

Kaylee rubbed her face, exasperated at the very thought. "Each patient who comes in takes at least two hours, in and out, sometimes more. That's time we could be giving to patients who are in more critical need. Many of these patients don't have a primary care physician because they're uninsured. They then get bills that are outrageously expensive, and more times than not, go unpaid. They get sent to collections and we have a department just for making collections calls for the next ninety days. By then, the amount of time and money we've spent on this one patient is huge. All for something that could have been treated at home."

"It sounds like you could use a better way to triage patients before they ever get to the hospital," Fatima said.

"At this point, I'd take any suggestions," Kaylee said.

"What if a nurse could triage people over the phone and let them know what they could do at home or whether or not they needed to come in?" Fatima responded.

"We have an advice nurse, but a lot of people would rather drive down and have someone look at them in person."

"But now you can see people in person, over the phone." Gordon held up his smartphone. "They just have to snap a picture and email it to the advice nurse. So many people have this capability on their phones, and in my opinion, the tech is going to be more widespread and more cheaply available in the next few years."

"That's actually a good suggestion," Kaylee said.

"We're not a software company, as you know, but what if we developed some consumer grade testing equipment? A blood pressure cuff, pulse oximeter, or a glucose meter?" Gordon asked.

"That could make a big difference," Fatima said slowly, thinking it over. "If people used the equipment, and maybe combined that with photos, we could tell a lot over the phone. We could help people before they even left their homes."

On the way back to MedTech Fatima said, "Is that really something you could do? I can see that being a great thing to offer my other customers."

"I'd have to check with Clete about using the new HL-7 protocol and see what he thinks about some consumer grade products, but yeah, I don't see why not. In a hospital setting getting the right data to the right person at the right time could mean the difference between life and death in some cases, so I'd think Clete would be interested in helping out."

Chapter 10
July 2008

Gordon dragged a chair up to Clete's desk and pulled two sandwiches out of a brown paper bag.

"Did you get my chips?" Clete asked, unwrapping his sandwich.

"Of course," Gordon produced the bright green bag and tossed it to his friend. "I don't know how you eat those."

"I'll have you know dill pickle is a very popular flavor." Clete pulled open the bag and tossed a handful of chips into his mouth to prove the point.

Gordon shook his head, laughing to himself as he bit into his sandwich. This weekly lunch had turned out to be beneficial on several levels. He genuinely enjoyed the company of his sometimes grumpy, but always insightful friend. Clete, also a Portland transplant, enjoyed their occasional bragging contest to see who could outdo the other's Midwest winter horror stories. But Clete had also become a valuable ally at work, helping Gordon understand an important segment of the company better.

"Hey," Clete said between bites, "I've been hearing whisperings that MedTech is talking to United Medical about a possible buyout. Do you know anything about that?"

Gordon shook his head while he struggled to swallow his last bite. He gulped. "No. I don't. Where did you hear that?"

"I was talking with the VP of engineering, and he mentioned they were waiting to make a decision on some new equipment until they knew more about how negotiations were going." Clete emphasized the word *negotiations*. "He kind of clammed up after that, like he said something he shouldn't have."

"Huh." Gordon's mind worked. If the company was waiting to make large purchasing decisions, something big was probably in the works.

"Changes could be coming." Clete cocked his head to the side, shrugging as he dug into his bag of chips.

"It could be nothing, or it could be something. We won't know until it happens," Gordon said, sagely. Despite this, a small seed of uncertainty planted itself in his mind and quickly grew into something he couldn't ignore. He stopped by Linda's HR office later that afternoon to see if he could dig for details.

"Between you and me," Linda said, "I don't know much. But I do know they've been in talks for several months," she confirmed. "I had to pull some numbers for them early on, otherwise I wouldn't know anything. Since then, they've kept it pretty quiet." She exhaled. "And you should too. We don't need a bunch of rumors flying around."

"I won't say anything," Gordon said. "It's good to have a little heads up, just in case." Linda nodded but didn't say anything. Her smile masked concern and Gordon wasn't sure if it was for him or for her. He decided not to ask.

* * *

True to his word, Gordon kept quiet about the acquisition talks...after filling Clete in on the details he'd learned from Linda, of course. Still, rumors spread, and it wasn't long before everyone knew something was going on. Work moved forward, but morale took a hit and more than once Gordon heard the word *resume* and *update* floating around the office talk.

The announcement came three weeks later, via email, that the buyout was complete and MedTech would be changing to United Medical, effective immediately. There were a few action items, but above all, they were instructed, everyone should go forward with business as usual. For most employees, the email explained, the only difference would be the name of the company that issued their paycheck. They would continue to manufacture the same products, work with the same coworkers and, in many cases, have the same managers. Things would continue with as little disruption as possible, the email, signed by CEOs from United Medical and MedTech, claimed.

Gordon let out a dark chuckle. Deniz Armen, MedTech's CEO was now the *former* CEO. He briefly wondered if there was a place for him in the merged company.

A second email appeared in Gordon's inbox just after the company announcement, this one addressed to upper-level employees only. It invited Gordon to a special meeting later that afternoon. He read through the names on the email address line and his stomach tightened. Something was coming, but at least he wouldn't be alone.

Rows of chairs were set up in one of the meeting rooms and Deniz and the CEO of United Medical stood at the front of the room. Gordon quickly found a seat next to Colin. "Should I start updating my resume?" he leaned over and said.

"The way I see it," Colin said, "there are a few ways this could play out, but most scenarios don't look good for those of us at our level."

Gordon exhaled, trying to let his tension go.

"Thanks for coming today. I know you probably have a lot of questions, but we wanted to keep you in the loop on what will be happening." Deniz shuffled papers on the podium in front of him. "I want to start by introducing Celia Castelluci, United Medical's CEO."

Celia stood and approached the podium while Deniz continued to speak.

"Celia has been with United Medical for eight years, the last three as CEO. In addition, she's managed two other acquisitions, so she is familiar with this process, and I know you will be in good hands with her and her team."

Gordon did not feel like he was in good hands.

There was an awkward transition as Deniz sat down and Celia took over the meeting. "As we bring MedTech into the United Medical family, I want you to know that this facility will still operate just as it currently is...with a few exceptions."

"I have a feeling I know what those exceptions are," Colin said under his breath.

"I'm sure it won't come as a total surprise to learn that, unfortunately, our need for upper-level management at this facility is greatly reduced as United Medical already has a strong team in place."

A low rumble of discordant voices broke the rapt silence, but Celia was quick to get things under control and it became clear that yes, she did have experience with acquisitions, but also with laying off large groups of high-level executives.

"We realize this is not the news you want to hear, but nothing is happening right away. We want to give you time to transition to your next place of employment, while you help us transition our new team into place. So, you've got a job here at United Medical for the next ninety days." Small eruptions of grumbles popped up around the room, but Celia continued. "We understand if you need to go elsewhere, but as an incentive to stay through the ninety days, we have a generous severance package. We'll be sending more details about that later today."

Gordon thought of his mortgage and car payments. He wanted to call Tricia and talk things through; he felt a surge of adrenaline, but forced himself to stay seated while the meeting continued. He heard Colin let out a long, low breath and looked to his boss, not for answers, but to ground himself. He wasn't alone.

"What are you going to do?" he asked Colin.

"I'll need to look at the severance package and see if it makes sense to stay," Colin said. "Of course, I don't have any irons in the fire right now, so I'm not going anywhere yet." He pushed off the arms of his chair, like standing took effort, weighed down with this new information.

As they filed out of the meeting room, Gordon wanted nothing more than to return to his office, shut the door and call Tricia, but as soon as he came back into the IT department, he was descended on by his team.

"What's happening?" Javier asked. "Are they letting us all go?"

"Are they kicking us out now?" Duane asked.

"No, no." Gordon waved his hand though the air. "You're all safe. No one is going anywhere, unless you want to." Duane and Javier followed him as he returned to his office. "I, on the other hand, have ninety days..."

Duane groaned.

"Noooo." Javier turned the word into lament.

"What are you talking about?" Claire popped her head in the office. "Are we getting fired?"

Duane pulled her in and shut the door behind her. "Not us," he said.

"I'm staying on to help the new IT director transition, and then I'll be let go." He tried to keep any emotion from his voice. Anger, sorrow, fear; he tried not to give them a place in the discourse. This was business.

Claire, Duane, and Javier's protests and complaints about fairness were not helping.

"I'll work with United Medical's IT group, but at the end of the day they're going to take it over," he said. "They've been transparent about that fact. They'll need to know how this department is run and what I've done with help desk and infrastructure management."

"That sucks," Claire said.

Gordon could not disagree.

"You've worked so hard to get IT respectable again," Duane said. "We had no credibility before you got here."

"And you'll still have credibility when I'm gone," Gordon said. "The processes are in place. You've got a services catalog and help desk protocol. You've been trained on ITIL. You have all the tools you need."

The three of them seemed to come to a reluctant acceptance.

"United Medical asked me to document everything that we've done. They want to know what our processes are, how we manage change management, what kind of helpdesk we run, and what our service catalog includes. I'll be working on gathering and documenting everything, but I imagine I'll need your help, too."

"That will take a while," Duane said.

"Well, we've got ninety days. We've got metrics we are generating for the company on a regular basis, so everyone knows what we're doing."

Claire nodded but her mouth twisted into a scowl.

"Listen," Gordon said. "You are the backbone of the IT department. You're the ones who did the work to build back trust in the IT department. And I'm still here for three more months. You haven't gotten rid of me yet." Joking about it helped a little.

* * *

The waitress set the mushroom burger and fries in front of him, and Gordon poured a healthy amount of ketchup on the side of his plate. Across from him, Colin dumped barbeque sauce on his chicken sandwich.

"You've got to get on LinkedIn," Colin said. "It's a good tool for networking."

"Are companies really using that?" Gordon said as he stuck a fry in his mouth.

"If they're not now, they will be soon." Colin dug into his own side of fries. "Get your photo up, list your job history, and start making connections. Networking. It's all about networking."

"Seems like one more social media time suck."

"Just do it," Colin said, turning his attention to his drippy sandwich.

Gordon shook his head and looked off into the distance before returning his focus to Colin. "I've got a meeting with the new IT director this afternoon about the transition. I won't lie. It's not going to be easy to just hand this department over to someone else. It feels like my baby. I don't want to just let it go."

"I get that. But everything you've done here speaks very well of you," Colin assured him. "You've got this great experience under your belt with actual numbers to prove you're the real deal. That's not nothing."

"I guess that's one way to look at it," Gordon said.

"That's resume gold, right there."

Colin had a good point. The metrics he'd been tracking would show to a future employer just what he could do.

Colin wiped some barbeque sauce off the corner of his mouth. "Mergers and acquisitions happen all the time. This is your first, but it may not be your last. Try not to take it personally. I know it still hurts, but it's business."

"I'm still going to be out of a job in ninety days." Gordon took a drink of his soda and looked at his watch.

"Shouldn't be for long," Colin said. "Get that networking going and you'll be fine. Speaking of which, I'm going to a Healthcare Information Management Systems Society meeting next week. Have you been yet?"

Gordon shook his head.

"You should come. I can introduce you to a few people and you can meet a few more. It's a great place to network for careers in health care. You need to be doing that now, more than ever."

* * *

The weeks flew by as Gordon worked to help the IT department transition to the new IT Director and CIO. He'd assumed his last ninety days would be a little cushy, but he couldn't have been more wrong. He was still acting IT director, busy organizing information and briefing the new CIO. The job search took up his time after work as he built a LinkedIn profile, updated his resume, posted it online, and scoured local job listings in the job boards. Several times a month he attended networking meetings and while they were definitely productive, he often came home feeling sapped of energy.

His last day at work, October 1, was fast approaching and he felt anxious that his job search wasn't further along. Colin had already gone on several interviews, while Gordon had yet to land his first. United Medical offered a nice severance package that would thankfully keep him insured and receiving a paycheck through the end of the year, but up until now, Tricia had insisted he only look for local jobs so they wouldn't have to uproot the kids. He couldn't wait forever for the right job to open in Portland, though. Maybe it was time he looked out of state? Tricia would understand and if not, one of Gordon's specialties was managing change. So maybe it would be okay.

* * *

Gordon sat in the garden area of MedTech's inner courtyard enjoying the late summer sun, some of the leaves already turning bright crimson, orange, and yellow. He had enjoyed spending lunchtime here when the weather was good as well as enjoying this view from inside when the weather was bad. He tossed the trash from his lunch in one of the bins and headed back to his office. All that was left now was his exit interview with United Medical's CIO, boxing the things in his office, and saying his final goodbyes.

His team had had time to get used to the idea of him leaving, but it was still a little solemn in the office. A half-eaten chocolate sheet cake had been covered in foil in the break room and several people insisted he take it home to his kids. But they didn't need that much cake. No one did. Besides, Tricia would be thrilled with the going away gift everyone had pooled their money to get him: a weekend getaway at a Willamette Valley winery for the two of them.

Gordon returned to his office in time to meet Wilson, the new CIO, for their scheduled meeting.

"Looks like things are going well for your last day," Wilson said. "Sorry about this."

"It's not easy, but I understand," Gordon said. "This has been a great place to work and the team in this department is first rate. I hope you come to appreciate them as I have."

"If your records and the information you've provided are any indication of what this group is like, I have no worries," Wilson admitted. "I'm impressed with your organization. You clearly have a great helpdesk and services catalog. The reputation of the IT department speaks for itself."

"It was a challenge," Gordon admitted, "but I think we got to a really good place."

Wilson nodded, then added, "Is there anything you wish you'd had time to do while you were here?"

"The only thing we haven't addressed is governance," he said. "We didn't get a team put together and we could really use one. We've got a long list of projects, but we don't know the priority because we don't have governance in place."

Wilson made several notes and thanked him for his input, and Gordon was done.

* * *

Tricia had his favorite meal waiting for him at home that night and they sat at the table long after the last bite had been taken and the kids had run off to play. Gordon poured them each another glass of wine.

"So, what are you thinking?" Tricia said. "It seems like you're in a good position. You've made some strides on your job search."

"Not as far along as I'd hoped," Gordon said. "But you're right. Overall, I'm not in a bad place."

"This could be a good opportunity. It's a chance for you to take the next step in your career." She sipped her wine and set the glass down, reaching for his hand across the table.

"I really want to do something where I can be in a position to help people and make a difference," Gordon admitted.

"That's a good goal," Tricia said. "There should be plenty of opportunities like that."

"I think maybe that means I stay in health care."

"Well, you certainly have some good connections at some of the hospitals you worked with. That should help."

"Yeah, but it's not every day that a CIO position opens up." Gordon stacked the dinner dishes nervously before proceeding. "I may get a job that requires us to move."

"I know." Tricia sank her face into her hands and sucked in a breath before looking at Gordon again. "I know. But can we cross that bridge when we come to it? Can I just be in denial a little while longer?" She gave him a weak smile.

It was enough for now.

* * *

"Gordon, you remember Matt Scott from Blessed Heart?" Gordon had been excited to see Fatima at the monthly HIMSS meeting and now here was Matt, the lab manager he'd met on their sales calls.

"Of course I do. Hey, Matt." Gordon shook his hand vigorously. It was good to reconnect with someone from his old job. "How are you doing?"

"Things are going well," Matt said. "The new United Medical machines with the HL-7 technology are a dream. Everything works together seamlessly."

"That's really good to hear," Gordon said, and it was. Just because he was no longer with the company manufacturing the machines didn't mean he didn't feel a swell of pride for the improvements to the customer experience with their products.

"You know," Matt said, "I heard there's an opening for a CIO out in Hillsboro at Grace Hospital. You should apply. You've got a good grasp on the hospital environment and the needs of the industry."

"Good suggestion," Fatima chimed in. "You would be great in that position. I don't think it's been posted online yet, so you could get your resume in there first."

"That's a nice sized hospital," Gordon said, going from memory. "About one hundred and fifty beds, right?"

"Exactly. Not too big; not too small," Matt added. "I know the hospital administrator over there and would be happy to put a good word in for you.

"That would be fantastic," Gordon said. "Thank you."

Chapter 11
April 2009

"There you are!" Tom Tseng rose from his booth at the neighborhood pub and greeted Gordon as he closed the distance between them. One of the first people he'd reached out to after accepting the job at Grace Hospital had been his old mentor. Tom had immediately suggested they meet for a drink to catch up. "Congratulations on your new role. CIO for a hospital is really impressive." He pulled out Gordon's chair, took his seat, and pushed the happy hour menu across the table.

"It was all thanks to some of the connections I'd made from the hospital, and through HIMSS meetings," Gordon explained.

"I'm sure your excellent track record had something to do with the job offer, too." Tom took a sip from the pint the waiter had just deposited in front of him.

"Well, sure." Gordon laughed. "But I never would have heard about the opening if it weren't for networking. And I have you to thank for helping me to see the value of that."

"Fine, I'll take it," Tom said. "You were *all work* for a while there at Mama Meg's. That mindset can only take you so far. It's all about balance."

"I'll drink to that," Gordon said, lifting his glass.

"So," Tom said after their tots had arrived, "there's a lot of pressure working IT in a hospital."

Gordon nodded. "Yeah, but I've had some great experience at MedTech, so I'm fairly familiar with the industry."

"Well, yeah, that will help. But when you're actually at the hospital, it will be a little different. If something goes wrong, people's lives are on the line."

Gordon exhaled. This had come up in his interviews and he'd had time to think about it. Yes, IT at a hospital was a big deal. If the system went down, or if the wrong data went to the wrong patient...well, it would be way more serious than when Clete didn't get his engineering software fixed immediately. The true pressure of it seemed to settle into Gordon for the first time. He nodded at Tom but didn't say anything.

As if he could see the worry building, Tom said, "you just need to make sure you've got a contingency for everything. If the system goes down, you need a fallback plan. It's no different than any place, really, but yes, the stakes are higher." Tom dragged a tot through the fry sauce and stuck it in his mouth. "You'll be fine," he said as he chewed.

Gordon nodded and grabbed the last two tots for himself, arching his eyebrows triumphantly. He would just have to make sure he had a really good business continuity plan, and he knew just how to do that.

* * *

Fifteen minutes. That's how long it took Gordon to get to his new job at Grace. That was shorter than his drive to MedTech, and much shorter than his old Mama Meg's commute. Tricia was thrilled she didn't have to move, and Gordon was thrilled to be starting this new chapter in his career. The short commute was just icing on the cake. He'd thought a lot about what Tom had said and was determined to make sure plans were in place should anything go wrong.

Meeta, the COO, met him on his first morning and showed him to his new office. It was bigger than his office at United Medical and had a wall of west-facing windows that looked out onto the Coast Range. "It gets a little bright in here in the afternoon," Meeta said. "So this might help." She picked up a little box, about the size of her palm, and pressed a button. Shades automatically dropped, blocking the light but keeping most of the view visible.

"That will definitely come in handy," Gordon said, setting his bag down near his desk. This office didn't only have a nice leather couch. It also had a small conference table surrounded by six chairs. He was definitely moving up in the world.

They spent the morning on a tour of the hospital with Meeta introducing Gordon to some of the people he'd be working with. He silently thanked his old MedTech sales friend, Fatima, for teaching him a couple strategies for remembering people's names. He'd found it helpful as they'd gone on sales calls and it was coming in very handy now.

As they passed the nurses' stations, Gordon noticed bulky CRTs on all the desks and wondered if they'd talked about getting those replaced with newer flat screens. As they passed through the emergency department, he saw patients filling out pages of paperwork on clumsy clipboards and in the ICU he learned about the long wait times as different departments communicated with each other. He'd have to do a little more digging to be sure but he knew there was a better way.

Meeta stopped by the café and they ordered lunch. "I'm sure it's a little overwhelming," she said.

Gordon nodded. "Every first day is." The café was bright, with windows that looked out onto a little garden, and the food was surprisingly good.

"Our last CIO was focused mostly on infrastructure, which was fine, but a lot of the more strategic issues got put on the back burner. I'm hoping that you'll find a way for your team to balance both the small, everyday technology issues, as well as the infrastructure needs," Meeta said. "Like we talked about in the interview, we can't afford mistakes, so the infrastructure has to be set up for success. A big part of morale, though, is seeing that individual needs are met, too."

"I plan to meet everyone's needs," Gordon said. "I have a few tools for making sure I do that. But one of the first things I need to do is get to know some of the decision makers."

"I was going to suggest the same thing," Meeta said.

"Great. We're on the same page." Gordon mentally reviewed all the people he'd met and names he'd remembered from this morning to come up with the name of the facilities manager. "I think I'll start with Phillip," he said.

"That's a great idea. You'll want to work closely with him," Meeta approved. "You should know, he's meticulous at his job. Very detailed." She blew on a spoonful of soup. "In fact, it's because of the way he does his job that I'm able to sleep at night." She laughed and sipped her cooled soup from the spoon.

"Sounds like we'll get along very well, then," Gordon said. He made an appointment to sit down and talk, and the next day, made his way to Phillip's office in the basement. As he rode the elevator down, his mind flashed back to that day, years ago, in the basement of the Student Center when he rented his graduation gown and met Tricia. He remembered the moment he decided to stay and take the job with Ann. Suddenly, everything seemed surreal. That one decision had led him here, to the position of Chief Information Officer of a whole hospital when he just as easily could be running the family farm today if he'd made a different choice. While he'd learned many valuable lessons in the last twenty years about how to be an IT leader, now, before he got to Phillip's office, he found himself reverting back to his old Business Analyst mindset. That's what it was really all about—understanding customer needs and meeting them with technology. And whether that customer was his own department, his company, or the clients and vendors his company worked with, it all came back to this.

"Come on in," Phillip said when Gordon arrived at his office. "How are you settling in?"

"Well, it's just my second day, but so far, so good." They exchanged small talk for another minute or two and Gordon found out Phillip was also a fan of professional soccer. They took a moment to speculate over rumors of the return of the Timbers, Portland's first ever professional soccer team, as part of the expansion of the Major League Soccer organization.

Meeta had accurately described Phillip when she called him meticulous. His desk was tidy, with everything arranged at right angles. Four identical pens stood at attention in a silver pen cup, his keyboard looked to be crumb-free, which either meant it was brand new or there was a can of compressed air somewhere in this office. His blue, short sleeve button-down shirt looked professionally pressed and starched, an unusual look for someone who didn't have a public-facing job.

Gordon knew this wouldn't be the only time he sat down and talked with Phillip, but he wanted to start by asking about the one thing he was most concerned about. "I want to understand some of the backup systems we have in place in case of emergency. I need to know the protocols."

Phillip nodded and explained their system. "We've got generators for power, but also battery backup so we've got a holdover until the generator starts up."

"That should help protect the equipment in the cutover," Gordon said.

Phillip nodded and took him to see the server room. Once again, Gordon appreciated his attention to detail. Everything in his realm was documented, tidy, and well organized.

They spent the whole morning together and in many of the rooms, Gordon noticed clipboards on the walls, documenting the thrice-daily equipment checks. A column of initials ran down one side of the sheets where one of the employees had signed off.

"We constantly monitor to make sure everything is running as it should," Phillip explained.

They finished the tour and Gordon reached out to shake Phillip's hand. "Thanks for your time. It's great to know I'll be working with someone so thorough. It will make my job easier."

"I feel the same way," Phillip said.

Wednesday Gordon spent time with Beau Willingham, the chief medical officer. He worked with the hospital staff doctors, as well as doctors with admitting privileges, and had a great feel for the community of physicians Gordon would need to work with. Beau's white coat hung neatly from the back of his door on a hanger and medical books lined the shelves behind his desk. The silver streaks that ran through the hair at Beau's temples gave him an air of wisdom and dignity.

"I want to get an idea of the type of technology you and the other doctors need to do your jobs efficiently and effectively," Gordon said after initial pleasantries.

"Honestly, anything that would help us spend a little less time with each patient and get more out of it would be helpful," Beau said. "We're under a lot of pressure to get in and get out of each patient visit. If we can see more patients, then we can bill more." He shrugged. "It's not pretty, but it's the truth. And we get hounded about it all the time."

Gordon took notes and shared his initial thoughts for solutions with Dr. Willingham, but promised to continue to think about the problem. With Tom Tseng's words still fresh in his mind, Gordon asked Dr. Willingham about the hospital's contingencies and emergency plan, continuing to scrawl everything down into his notebook. He'd understood the hospital's need to increase billing. They were a business, after all. But something felt off about making it so doctors could spend less time with patients.

The nurses, on the other hand, were a different story. They were with patients constantly. The director of nursing, Alberta Kaye, wore white scrubs, her name badge clipped to the hem of her top, hanging freely at her hip. She was all business. Gordon followed her back to her office Thursday afternoon, her white clogs squishing as she walked. Just because she was with Gordon didn't keep her from issuing commands to the various stations they passed.

"Look at this outdated tech," she said, pointing to the CRT. "I know we're a small hospital, but the nurses at Good Sam downtown have flat screen monitors. When patients and visitors come in here, these monitors set a tone, you know? They say, "This is an old hospital with old technology and they're probably going to treat me with outdated methods.""

A smile crept on to Gordon's face as he considered Alberta's logic.

"If you boil it right down, nurses do ninety percent of the care," Alberta said, veering away from the computer monitors and leading him down another hall. "I need to make sure my staff are happy. Whatever they need, I try to give them."

"I understand," Gordon said.

"Do you?" Alberta asked and Gordon straightened at the question, turning to give the woman his full respect and attention. This was why she was the Director of Nursing. "Does this mean you're going to get us new computers?

Whole computers? Gordon looked at her critically and then saw right through her. He saw what she was trying to do. Very sly. "I will put flat screen monitors at the top of my list," he said carefully, scribbling something in his notebook.

Alberta smiled. "While you're at it, we could really use the ability to see what's going on with each patient, confirm orders, see what is scheduled in terms of care or medication, and be able to track who ordered everything."

Gordon felt like she was a pump that had just been primed, ideas flowing from her faster and faster. He listened, asking questions for clarification when he needed it, and as he said goodbye at the end of their meeting, he knew Alberta Kaye, with her vast knowledge and her close work with patients and nurses, was someone he needed to stay close to.

He met with the lab manager, who talked about how she'd love a way to make sure all the data they gathered doing their lab work got to nurses and physicians quickly and accurately. "Everyone needs to be on the same page, from the doctors to the pharmacists, so we can make sure each patient is getting the right care and mistakes are not made."

In the imaging department, Gordon took special note of all the technical equipment they worked with and the size of the images they were producing. "How do you get your images to the right people?" Gordon asked.

"Right now, we develop the image and then someone hand delivers it to the right department."

"You have to process every one? That sounds like it takes a lot of time."

"Well, that's how we've always done it. It would be great if we could send images electronically, but the files are just too big."

Gordon's mind worked. He'd have to upgrade the networks if they wanted to be able to do that. He made a few more notes. Many of the concerns people expressed had to do with moving data around the hospital. A new HIS system would make that process easier and more efficient. He added it to his list. But there was something more that he couldn't let go. Something in the back of his mind.

A lot of the comments he'd heard were focused on the overall success of individual departments. But the lab manager had been one of the first to suggest that the patient experience should be what they should focus on. Gordon knew from his experience with Blessed Heart and his dealings with his old friend, Matt Scott, that a patient-centric model would ultimately prove more successful than a department-centric one. That's where governance would come in. They'd need to make investments based on the best thing for the patient and the success of the hospital would naturally follow.

* * *

"You've sure been getting around," Meeta said over lunch one day. "Everyone I talk to has had your undivided attention at one point or another over these last few weeks. I have to say, they really appreciate being heard. It means a lot that you've listened to their concerns. Now, I just hope you have a plan to address those concerns." There was hope mixed with warning behind her smile. It might have looked like Gordon was not producing much and maybe she wondered if she'd made the right hiring decision. But there was no use jumping into this job just to do all the wrong projects. It was crucial to get started on the right foot.

"The challenge I see is that everyone is worried about what they can do quickly and easily. They sometimes forget about the patient."

Meeta nodded. He had her attention now.

"When you see a patient for the first time, they fill out paperwork. That goes in a file and every time they come in, more paper gets added to the file. If decisions need to be made about the patient, you pull the file. Then, when another doctor needs to understand something about the patient, they have to request the file and someone has to physically deliver it. So, you have these big, fat patient files that are constantly being pulled and refiled."

"It's not ideal, but it's worked for us for a long time," Meeta said. "It might be inefficient, but we make it work."

"It's not just that it's inefficient. It's more prone to errors. What happens if that patient file is misplaced? Filed in the wrong spot? What happens if a pharmacist misreads a doctor's handwriting and prescribes the wrong meds?"

Meeta's eyes narrowed as she followed his line of thinking. She knew this was the case, but hadn't really focused on solutions to the problem.

"After the intake forms, there should be no more paperwork. It should be all electronic. When the patient moves from department to department, or comes from an outside clinic, they shouldn't have to fill out any more paperwork. All the basics like insurance, prescriptions, diagnoses, treatments... everything should be carried along with the patient and available immediately to whoever needs to see it in the hospital."

"That sounds like something we should focus our efforts on here. I'm looking forward to Grace having this sort of system in place in the future," Meeta said.

"It's not the future," Gordon said. "It's happening right now. Electronic health records are starting to roll out and we could adopt them. It might require a switch over to a new HIS but this technology is available now."

"I'd need to know what something like that costs before approving it," Meeta said. "It sounds expensive."

"Well, I wouldn't want just your approval."

She narrowed her eyes again, confused. "You do remember I'm the COO," she said with a smirk.

"We need to set up governance; a team with someone representing each department who can speak up for their interests. Decisions need to be made together. It's crucial that everyone agrees on which projects are most important before we start implementing anything."

"You're already attending our weekly meetings, but you've been pretty quiet. Maybe you need to take a bigger role?"

"The weekly meetings are important, but they're more tactical than strategic. What I need to discuss is strategy and the weekly meeting would be a great place to start doing that."

"Well, then. Let's make it happen." Meeta said.

Chapter 12
August 2009

Voices rose in the hospital conference room, just skirting the edge of civility. The plate of scones in the center of the table sat untouched. Gordon had gotten used to the familiar tension of rolling out governance and the process always started the same way—with a lot of bickering. "I'm still having problems getting all the lab equipment to talk to each other," Olga, the lab manager, said. "I'm stuck in this limbo where not all of the systems are integrated, so we end up having to still rely on data entry for some things. And training is a mess because every time I train my employees on a new procedure, they are forced to revert to the old way for the remaining processes that aren't yet fully integrated. If anything, it's less efficient than just doing everything the old way."

"That's a big issue we need to address," Gordon said. "All systems should be HL-7 compatible, but as I'm sure you're aware, it's not like flipping a switch. This is a huge data migration, and it will take time to get one hundred percent operational."

Alberta chimed in. "Our nurses have been waiting for new equipment for years. We've got the oldest computers in the hospital. We've still got CRTs, while you all have flat screens. Granted, this might not be as critical as integrating all the lab equipment," she conceded. "But our CPUs are so slow, it takes forever just to download emails. We don't have time to sit around waiting for lab reports. These are critical minutes that may mean the difference between life and death."

Gordon nodded as he took notes. "I hear that. New equipment should be a relatively easy fix. That may be something we want to address first."

"If any department is going to get IT's attention, it should be the pharmacy," said Yumi, the head pharmacist. "The amount of paperwork associated with the meds we dispense, plus the stuff the FDA and the health authority want—it's a lot of paperwork. We have to make sure that everything we dispense is recorded and has a sign-off from someone who has the authority to prescribe. If we could start barcoding it would make it easier to keep track of what we've got in stock."

"Be that as it may," Alberta said, "if you deliver prescriptions any slower, we're going to have to start calling out to the Walgreens down the street. I'm pretty sure they could beat your time, even if you count having to drive there to pick up." She shook her head, her good-natured laugh lessened the sting of her words, but the arch of her eyebrows made it clear there was truth to her criticism. Alberta uncapped her water bottle and took a sip.

Yumi tried to massage the worry out of her forehead. "We've had a lot of turnover lately and I'm training three new techs. I realize we've been slow, but just be patient with us and things will pick up once these guys get settled."

Gordon directed a questioning look to Dr. Beau Willingham, waiting for his input.

The doctor shrugged. "I need to talk with the doctors and get their input, but I can tell you I'm real hesitant to disrupt our current flow, which I think is good."

A chorus of murmurs from everyone else made clear that not everyone agreed.

"I don't mean the data flow, or the flow of meds from the pharmacy," Beau quickly amended and Yumi rolled her eyes. "As far as the doctors' workflow goes, we don't have any complaints."

"You know why that is, don't you?" Alberta said blankly as she stiffened.

"I know," Beau said. "I understand how much work goes on behind the scenes to make our jobs run seamlessly. Truly, I do." His voice was sincere, and Alberta relaxed. "I'm just telling you what the typical doctor's perspective is and their reaction will probably be, *If it ain't broke, don't fix it.* Even the littlest change disrupts things. A big change, well, that would be a hard sell." Beau used a napkin to grab a scone and took a bite, punctuating the end to his part in this conversation.

"This is good feedback, Beau. Thank you," Gordon said. "I think we can all agree, though, that we want what's best for the hospital as a whole." Beau nodded. "And I think we can all agree, we'll resolve the issues most successfully if we don't try and work on them all at once." More heads nodded. "What I suggest—and what has worked at other companies I've worked for—is what's called an IT steering committee."

Alberta scoffed. "Sounds like just one more meeting. I don't have time to spend all day in meetings." A few others mumbled the same complaint.

"The steering committee would be made up of each department's decision makers, so yes, you'd need to come to another meeting, but it will be well worth your time."

There was more muttered pushback.

"I don't like meetings that waste my time either," Gordon said. "But as a steering committee you can evaluate which projects get focus first. The IT department only has so many resources and we can be most effective if we're using our resources in the right way. Trust me." Gordon thought of all the times he'd made this promise before, and all the times he'd delivered. He would do so, again. "IT's goal is to make your jobs run more efficiently and make things easier for you, so all of these projects should ultimately help everyone. We just need a consensus on what project to prioritize."

Meeta, who, up to this point, had simply observed, looked impressed when several people, including Alberta, nodded their agreement. At the head nurse's acceptance, Yumi and Beau added theirs. It was a good start and Gordon would take it.

Later, after everyone had left, Meeta commented on the shift in thinking. "I certainly didn't see you turning that group around so quickly," she said.

"I wouldn't say they're completely turned around, but it's a good first step." Gordon smiled confidently. What they were giving him was a chance—a chance to prove that his methods could work. He was right smack in the middle of the IT pyramid again, building relationships with his internal customers. If he could win over crusty old Clete, he was pretty sure this group would see the wisdom in his plan as well. He got the first IT steering committee meeting on the calendar for the next week and got to work preparing for it.

For the IT department to be as successful as possible, they needed to know where they currently stood in several different areas. To determine that, Gordon needed an IT score card. Unlike the IT survey he'd done at MedTech, the score card included numbers on how all the systems were working, including the time that systems were operational and the status of projects in progress. Grace Hospital already had a successful IT department and help desk, so there was actual data to pull from. The score card was useful internally, but it would also be a valuable tool for the IT steering committee. Heads of each department would see the importance of the work they were doing, and it would give a real starting point to measure their progress on their strategic projects.

"Everything I'm doing right now has to do with building internal relationships," he told Meeta while they caught up at lunch. "Your last CIO was focused on infrastructure, which is great because there's a solid set-up already in place. This gives me the opportunity to bring the strategic needs of the hospital together under a technology umbrella."

"I get that," Meeta said, taking a bite of her pasta salad. Her phone buzzed and she checked the notification and set it back down on the table, returning her focus to Gordon.

"My next step is to find out how to best use technology to meet the strategic needs of the hospital."

"I trust that you know what you're doing," she told him. "I support you completely. But…" she trailed off.

"But?" Gordon prodded.

"But," she finally said, "you'll have your work cut out for you with some of these doctors. They get very set in their ways. Not only that," she exhaled, as if she were considering her words carefully. "Some of them might think they are the most important thing at this hospital. And it's true, we couldn't operate without the talented doctors on our staff, but they tend to forget that it takes more than just people with advanced medical degrees to make this hospital run. Some of them might feel like their opinion holds more sway."

This was nothing new. There was always going to be pushback whenever change was proposed. Whether it was Walt at Mama Meg's or Clete at MedTech, or many others who just didn't want to learn a new way of doing things, everyone had their reasons to dig in. He got it, though. Change was hard. That's why a big part of his job was managing that change; making it more palatable; easing people through it with as little disruption as possible.

"I feel like Beau is on board. He'll be a good advocate with the other doctors," Gordon said, stabbing for the cherry tomato in his salad.

"Yes, he will," Meeta said, looking at the time on her phone.

Gordon realized he needed to get back to work, too, and gathered his plastic utensils and wadded-up paper napkin for the trash. "One more thing," he said before getting up. "What do you know about this slowdown in the pharmacy? I worry something might go wrong before she's able to get the new techs up to speed, and if there's a way to anticipate something and come up with a fix..."

Meeta cut him off. "I'm keeping an eye on things and Yumi has it under control. She's hired some very sharp techs, but they're starting at an incredibly busy time. I appreciate your thinking about it, though. I can let you know if anything changes."

He kept this at the forefront of his mind as he went into his first steering committee meeting the next week. Gordon didn't waste time and got started off with his score card. It detailed which projects were on time, or in *green* status, and which were in *yellow* or *red*. It listed *up* time for all the systems and network, as well as help desk performance. By looking at the score card, anyone could easily see if IT was meeting their agreements on time and the rate of customer satisfaction. Gordon even included a section detailing IT employee turnover rate, which he felt was a barometer for the overall health of the IT department.

"This is impressive." Alberta flipped the paper over and back again. "It's a lot of good information on one page. I could use something like this for my nurses."

"It will evolve over time to include more," Gordon said. "But the idea is that you can know at a glance how IT is doing and if we are meeting our goals—goals set by *this* committee in *this* meeting, and the ones to follow."

Phillip nodded. He looked like he appreciated the organized and easily digestible sets of data. "This will keep everyone accountable."

"Well, it's designed to build up confidence in the IT department, but yes, this information will also help us as a committee keep track of our progress." Gordon tapped his stack of papers against the conference table and turned on the overhead projector. "Now, let's discuss the different projects we need to consider."

"I should mention," Beau said, "the doctors I talked to have brought up some concerns and I think they make a good point. We're in the business of filling beds. We need to make sure that we don't make changes that would negatively affect that."

"Of course," Gordon said.

"I mean, I realize that we're here to make positive changes for the hospital as a whole, but let's not forget that we're ultimately here to care for and cure as many people as we can."

"I agree," Alberta said. "But we also need to have the technology in place to deal with more full beds. Updating the nurses' computers would help that happen."

"I agree that should be a priority," Gordon said.

Alberta shot him a grateful smile. "Thank you." "And it seems like a project that should be able to be completed fairly quickly." Gordon laid out a proposed timeline and budget that everyone quickly agreed to. "In fact, we may even be able to start a second project while we're waiting for the computers to arrive. We just have to make sure to schedule time for the install."

"What should the next project be, then?" Yumi asked.

"I'd like to propose updating the Hospital Information System." Gordon watched for reactions, trying to take the temperature of the room. "You are probably all aware that there's talk of major health care reform on a national level, and we need to be ready for whatever's coming. It could be a game changer."

Beau scoffed. "They've been trying to get health care passed since the Clinton administration," he said. "Everything is still very much up in the air. Should we really plan on something that may not ever happen? We need to think about how we can see more patients."

Gordon listened. The doctors held sway at the hospital and if he didn't get them on board, he would have a hard time getting buy-in from other departments as well. He needed to win over Beau. "It seems like if we build better relationships with our feeder channels like the clinics, maybe bring in more admitting physicians, it would go a long way toward ensuring our beds are full." Beau nodded and Gordon continued. "Beyond that, we probably need to make sure we've got home health care or long-term health care relationships set up for post-care?"

"Exactly," Beau said. "Primary care, secondary, specialists, tertiary, post tertiary. We need to focus on building up all of those relationships."

"The way I see it," Gordon said, "we'll be in a better position to do that if we're able to move patient information and data across those channels smoothly. That's where an HIS comes in. That will ultimately help build up a feeder and post tertiary network. If we can successfully install a new HIS everything will be integrated. Moving patients from one care facility to another will be more efficient than ever. And it will also be safer. Patient information travels with the patient. No more pulling files and sending them by courier. It's all on one system. Mistakes will be reduced, and the hospital becomes a more patient-centric environment. It's the right thing to do for the patients, but also, ultimately, the best thing for the doctors, too."

"This makes sense to me," Yumi said, and Olga, the lab manager, nodded in agreement.

"I agree," Beau conceded. "Understand, though, that I have to bring this information back to all the doctors and sell it to them."

"I see how that might be a tall order," Gordon said. "Would it help to remind them about how patient records are all over the place right now? Some are in HIS, but some are still on paper."

"That's right," Olga said. "Diagnostics, for example, are completely separate. It would make things much more efficient to have the records all in one place."

"That kind of thing affects every one of us," Alberta said, and the others agreed. "And who knows, but getting more fully integrated with an HIS will make things faster for the pharmacy, too." She side-eyed Yumi.

"I explained this last week, Alberta." Yumi was not amused. "I've had a lot of turnover. The new techs are coming along well, though. We've been slammed and between training and filling prescriptions, it's been slow going."

"Well, I hope they're quick learners. Don't you have a few vacation days coming up next month?" Beau said. "They'll need to be up to speed."

Yumi assured him, "They'll be fine. Plus, the night shift pharmacist is filling in for me while I'm gone. It will be fine."

"Is there a way IT might be able to help?" Gordon asked. "There are things we could do to help your processes be more efficient."

Yumi shook her head. "Updating the HIS will help us most. Honestly, it's just getting past training these new hires," she said. "It's a bit of a perfect storm, I'm afraid." She looked at Alberta. "But like I said, if you all can be patient for a little longer, we're doing our best."

Alberta shrugged and Gordon thought he saw he roll her eyes. "Let's talk about the HIS, then," he said. "I think in the long run, this is the project that will benefit all of us in some way." Gordon filled in the details about what an HIS project might look like and answered all their questions. At the end, he called for an informal vote. Beau was a reluctant aye, but with his vote, the consensus was unanimous. Everyone wanted to move ahead with the HIS project after getting new computers for the nurses. And with that, the first steering committee meeting was in the books.

* * *

Gordon spent the next few weeks working with his IT team to organize the upcoming projects. The nurses' computers arrived and were installed without too much trouble, but the real IT focus was on coming up with a plan for the HIS implementation. One of the biggest challenges was ensuring that internal departments were passing patient information efficiently and effectively. The system would also have to manage requests from vendors and outside agencies who wanted to connect with them. It was crucial that the HIS was flexible enough to accept data from other systems easily.

"It's critical that we figure out a way to get data in a standardized form," Gordon said to Beau a few weeks later as they shared lunch in his office. The head doctor had been championing the steering committee's plans and his efforts were paying off. Most of his opposition came from some of the more senior doctors who had no desire to learn a new way of doing things so close to retirement.

"The doctors are on board with normalizing the ICD codes they use on patient charts. It will take some getting used to, but they're making an effort," Beau said. "The challenge we have here is our outside entities, doctors with admitting privileges, aren't getting the same level of support to make these changes. Plus, they have their own suggestions and opinions for how to do things. It's going to take some communication."

"It's not just the admitting doctors. We've got to have consistent communication between all departments," Gordon said. "Pharmacy, radiology, labs...they all need to be on the same page."

Just then, Alberta stormed into Beau's office. "We've got a big problem," she said. "One of the nurses just noticed the pharmacy sent the wrong meds for the patients for at least this morning's shift."

Beau pounded his desk and swore. "How did this happen? Where's Yumi?"

"She's out this week. Another pharmacist is filling in."

"That the one who switched from night shift?" Gordon asked.

Alberta nodded. "I'm pretty sure we caught it before any of the patients actually took the wrong medication. Thank goodness Martha was paying attention and noticed one of the patients was getting an emetic when they should have been getting pain meds. We stopped and checked everything. All the right prescriptions and doses were there, but the names were all wrong."

"So, we've got a pharmacist who normally sleeps during the day supervising a day shift of brand-new techs?" Beau shook his head, incredulous.

"Meeta is down there now, but it sounds like they got backed up and didn't follow all the procedures exactly, but we're still trying to find out exactly where the breakdown happened, so it doesn't happen again."

"She needs to provide more support to Yumi until things get better," Beau said, his anger transitioning right into indignation.

"I knew something like this was going to happen," Alberta said. "I've got to get back, but I wanted to keep you in the loop. We'll need to double and triple check all the meds for the foreseeable future."

Beau turned to Gordon. "At least until the HIS is fully implemented, right? This kind of thing won't happen when we've got the data flow working properly."

"Exactly. Once we've got the systems in place, there will be multiple fail safes so mistakes like that should essentially be eliminated."

Gordon returned to his office and got back to work on the HIS project.

Chapter 13
March 2010

"I've got the numbers for you," Fiona said. The hospital's IT manager had become indispensable as Gordon put together the HIS project presentation for the board and executive team. As soon as the project was approved, he knew she would make the perfect project manager.

"Thanks." Gordon took the file and flipped through it. "This looks great." Fiona had worked with the various departments to gather data for the last six months. The numbers quantified departmental operational activities and included information on the length of patient stays, medications prescribed, and any lab done on each patient. Alberta and Beau were getting him more specific numbers from their departments which would be critical for making his case for this multi-million-dollar project. In addition, he needed to be ready to explain all the benefits a new HIS would provide, as well as answer any questions the group might have. It was one thing to say this would make things better for everyone, but numbers couldn't lie. They would show without a doubt that the HIS would improve the patient experience and more than that, the hospital overall.

"The board would be crazy to not see the benefits of a new HIS," Fiona said. "And it has to be done at some point.

If we don't move on this now, we're going to be left behind, technology-wise."

"True. But the question they'll have to answer is whether or not to do it now or to wait. I need to convince them to do it now." Gordon turned when he saw Alberta at his door.

"I got you the information you wanted," she said.

"Perfect." Gordon reached out to take it.

"The flu cases from the last three years?" Fiona said when she saw what Alberta had brought.

"Exactly." Gordon accepted the file and quickly flipped through, stopping on the last page. "This is good," he said. "When I show the board how busy the hospital will be next fall and winter, it will demonstrate the urgency. If we don't start now," Gordon said, "we'll either have to wait another year, or we will run the risk of trying to get everyone trained on a new system when things are at their most hectic."

"It would be a nightmare," Alberta said.

"Exactly. But if we can get everyone up to speed before the height of flu season, we'll be set up for things to run more efficiently for everyone involved."

Gordon's administrative assistant popped his head into the office. "Tricia's on line one," he said. "Want me to take a message?"

Gordon shook his head. "I'll take it. Thanks for this," he gestured to Alberta with the stapled papers. "I'll let you know if I need anything else."

Alberta nodded and she and Fiona left the office.

"Hey, hon," Gordon said as he picked up the line.

"Jacob's game just got switched to the West Union field. Do you want to meet us there?"

These days his son lived and breathed baseball. His room was covered in posters of Felix Hernandez and when he wasn't playing catch with Gordon or neighborhood friends, he was practicing at a local indoor training facility. His hard work had paid off, earning him a position as one of the team's pitchers. Gordon couldn't have been more proud. "I better meet you there, just in case I don't get out of here right on time. I don't want you to be late on my account."

"Sounds good. I'll have a sandwich for you, so don't worry about dinner. Just get to the game."

It was still early in the season, but they were playing their rival tonight and Jacob had been nervous about it all week. Gordon didn't want to be late.

He ended the call and got back to the numbers for his presentation. He had no doubt the data were convincing, and as Fiona had said, a new HIS was only a matter of time. The board just needed to understand that now was the time. Not next year or the year after. Now. But he had to strike the right balance. If he came off too pushy, it could backfire. He needed a way to explain this to them so they would see the wisdom in acting now.

* * *

Gray clouds pressed down on the parents huddled under pop-up tents at West Union field. The emerald grass in the outfield had been mowed into a checkerboard grid. Gordon found Tricia handing out a sandwich and chips to Hannah while chatting with another mom. "Just in time," she said, handing Gordon his sandwich and leaning in to kiss him. "First inning's just about ready to start." He settled into the folding camp chair and located his son along the third-base line throwing fastballs into his catcher's mitt.

"How's he doing?" he asked, admiring his son's wind up. They'd worked for hours on his form in the backyard since the day after Christmas when he'd gotten the pitching target.

"He's looked great all through warm-up," she said. "But he's still nervous."

Gordon could tell the nervousness had spread to his wife. "He'll do great," he said. "You know how he gets in the zone."

"You're right," she said. "Hannah, get down from there!" Tricia jumped up and ran to coax Hannah down from a tree where she and several other of the younger kids were playing.

Gordon continued to watch Jacob throw knuckleballs to his teammate crouched in the dirt. The ump called *Play Ball!* and Jacob took his place on the mound. The first three innings came and went quickly, with no hits or runs as all the players, showing hopped up nerves, overthought every pitch, and either walked or struck out. It was the Little League version of a nail-biter. At the top of the fourth, Jacob took a few practice pitches, and the batter approached home plate. He was one of those kids whose growth spurt got the parents on the opposing team making casual comments about birth certificates and league rules.

Gordon could tell from his stance that he was ready to swing. "Be a hitter, Chase!" someone from the other team yelled. "Give it a ride!" Gordon sat forward in his chair, watching Jacob take the signal from the catcher. He nodded and threw. Not his best pitch, but Chase took a high swing, his bat chopping the air.

"Strike!" the umpire shouted, and Chase stepped back from the plate and took a couple of practice swings before approaching again.

Jacob adjusted his cap then stood ready, his hand holding the ball tucked into his mitt, looking over his left shoulder straight down the line at home plate. He wound up and let the ball fly, an outside pitch that Chase was determined to hit despite the fact that he had to lean forward to try and reach it.

"Stee-RIKE," the umpire sang out. The kid had missed, but Gordon blew out a breath. The power in that swing left no doubt that when this kid connected, the ball would be gone.

"Gotta be in your wheelhouse, buddy," someone shouted as Chase tapped his cleats with his bat and stepped back to the plate. All Jacob needed to do was throw anything that wasn't too far out of the box and this kid would swing for it. He went into his windup and let the ball fly. It sailed right over home plate.

No one was surprised when the kid swung and the crack from the ball connecting with the bat caused cheers to erupt from the spectators. The ball exploded off the bat, hard and fast, a line drive. Jacob reacted as fast as he could, but it would have required superhuman reflexes to avoid disaster. Everyone heard the dull thud when the ball hit Jacob's temple. It wasn't as loud as Chase's hit, but it was much more dramatic.

A few gasps peppered the crowd, and someone swore. Later, Gordon would realize it had been him. Tricia cried out and ran to the fence, her fingers laced through the links like she was ready to rip them down. Jacob's coach was out to the pitcher's mound in seconds and all the players on the field took a knee, stopping play.

He wasn't moving. Jacob wasn't moving.

The coach sought them out in the crowd and motioned for them to come out. Tricia ran, not waiting for Gordon, who was close behind. She reached him first and dropped to her knees in the mud. Jacob's eyes opened slowly and confusion read plainly on his face, along with a large red welt on the side of his head.

The assistant coach joined the huddle with a first aid kit, although there was not much to do besides cracking the ice-pack and pressing it to Jacob's head. Jacob tried to sit up but his coach stopped him. "What's your name, what day is today, can you move your fingers?" Coach asked, barely waiting for Jacob's answer to one before moving on to the next. "They made us all take concussion first aid training at the beginning of the season," he explained to Gordon and Tricia.

"I feel fine," Jacob said weakly, not fooling anyone.

"Let's get him off the field," Coach said. "You think you can walk, buddy?"

Jacob nodded and let his coach help him stand and support him as he walked off the field.

"He needs to be seen by a doctor. He's probably got a concussion, but they can do some further tests to be sure. Grace Hospital is just a few minutes away," Coach suggested.

"You take him," Tricia said. "I'll drop Hannah off with Lucy's family and meet you at the hospital in about twenty minutes."

Gordon buckled Jacob into the front seat and drove as carefully as he could, trying to minimize quick starts and stops as he made his way to Grace Hospital's Emergency Room. The admitting nurse smiled when he told her he worked with Alberta and handed him a clipboard and pen. "Don't forget to fill out the back, too," she said as he returned to Jacob and took one of the empty chairs. There were three different forms on the clipboard and right away Gordon knew his task was going to be difficult.

"Who is your primary care physician?" he asked Jacob. How did he not know this?

"Doctor Crockett," he said.

"Do you know his first name?" he asked, worried he was making Jacob think too much.

"No," Jacob said with a little effort and then moaned. "I feel sick," he said. "Like I might throw up."

Gordon got a small basin from the nurse and returned to his seat and back to the forms. He stopped at the next question. *Primary Care Physician Phone number*. How was he supposed to know his son's doctor's phone number off the top of his head? He skipped the question and moved on to the next one. *Insurance information*.

He checked the automatic doors at the entrance to the ER, willing Tricia to walk through them. She would know this stuff. He skipped that question too and moved on. Ah, *birthday*. That was one he could answer. He scribbled the numbers and moved on to the address section.

"January twenty-seventh," Jacob said.

"What?" Gordon said as he filled in his zip code.

"The twenty-seventh. Not the seventeenth. You got my birthday wrong."

Gordon looked at what he'd written. January seventeenth. That was right, wasn't it? "Are you sure?" Gordon had been there, after all.

"I know my own birthday," he said. "I didn't get hit that hard."

Gordon changed the one into a two and let out a sigh of relief when Tricia finally showed up.

"How are you doing? How long do we have to wait? Did they say anything about whether or not we need to be worried?"

"They handed me a fresh ice pack," Gordon said, remembering the crinkly pack in his pocket. He'd forgotten all about it since focusing on the paperwork. "You have to squish it to get it to work," he said.

Tricia huffed and took it from him. Within seconds she'd pressed it gently to the side of Jacob's head.

"Do you know the phone number for Doctor Crockett?" Gordon asked.

She had Jacob hold the ice pack and pulled a few cards out of her purse. "Here's Doctor Crockett's card. Here's our insurance information. What else do we need?"

Gordon scribbled down the information, deciding to just trust that Jacob did indeed know his birthday and not ask Tricia to confirm.

"Jacob Rusbart?" a nurse called from the doorway leading back to the exam rooms.

Tricia helped him stand while Gordon fumbled with his clipboard, pen, and lap full of cards and followed them into the back.

"I'll take that," the nurse said, holding out her hand for the clipboard.

"I'm not quite done filling it out," he said.

"That's okay. I'll finish it up for you. I've actually got some more paperwork for you to fill out. Jacob, you can have a seat on this bed. Feel free to lie down if you want. The doctor will be in soon." She thrust another clipboard into Gordon's hands.

Jacob's nausea seemed to subside, and his mood improved to the point where he started to get a little impatient with the process of the doctor and nurses examining him.

"It's great you're feeling fine, but that doesn't mean your brain is okay," the doctor said. "Based on what your mom said, I think we want to get an MRI, just to make sure there hasn't been a fracture." He turned to Gordon and Tricia. "I'll need to have one of the nurses call over there to check on availability, so until then, just hang tight." He lowered the lights in the room. "No TV for now. Just try to relax."

When they finally got to Imaging, Gordon had more paperwork to fill out. Tricia had gone home to get a toothbrush and a few other things for both Jacob and herself when it became clear they would be spending the night.

Hours later, as Gordon drove home and his concern for Jacob started to level out, his irritation over the whole process started to ramp up. He picked up Hannah from Lucy's and took her out to Burgerville for dinner. Once she knew Jacob was going to be okay, she seemed to be pretty happy with the one-on-one time she was getting with her dad. And the chocolate milkshake.

"Mom never lets us get milkshakes," she said.

Gordon smiled as he stole one of his daughter's fries and popped it in his mouth before she could stop him.

"Hey, that was mine," she said, aghast at his audacity.

"Dad tax," he said, smiling.

"Mom doesn't charge me Mom tax," Hannah said.

"But she also doesn't get you milkshakes," he pointed out, snatching one more.

"That's fair," Hannah said. "But that's the last one I'm going to let you take."

While his daughter sipped her shake, he continued to ponder his experience at the ER. Now he knew exactly what he was going to say to the board of directors to convince them to approve the HIS project.

* * *

A few days later in the conference room, the lights dimmed and Gordon clicked to the first slide of his presentation, a picture of Grace Hospital. The hospital board, Meeta, and the rest of the members of the executive team watched from their seats. "Last week my son got a concussion, and we made a visit to the ER here at Grace," he said, "and I experienced what it's like to be a patient at this hospital." All faces watched him expectantly, waiting for his next words. "I have to say, the care my son received was wonderful. From the admitting nurse to the doctor and nurses who spent time with us, I could tell that he was in good hands." There was a softening of the room as everyone let the praise wash over them.

"However," he said, "quality care is only part of the patient experience. During one of the most terrifying moments a parent can have, I had to fill out paperwork rather than focus on my son. And not just once. At several different points in the process, I was given additional forms to complete. Communicating between departments took hours. And when my son returned for a follow-up appointment after a few days, we had more paperwork to fill out.

If we want to keep up with the changing landscape in health-care, we need to create a more patient-centric experience and that is why we need a new HIS system in place." Gordon clicked through his slides until he came to a sample IT scorecard. "All of the data on this scorecard comes out of the HIS," Gordon explained. "This is the tool we use to gauge the hospital's financial health, details on the patient experience, what we are doing well, and how we can grow and make more money." He clicked through a few more slides to show more examples. "As you know, this is also the data that is used to assign our hospital rating. With a new HIS, we'll have more control over the numbers on this scorecard. And more control means we'll have better information on how to increase our HCAHPS rating." Eyes lit up. They liked that idea.

"In the future," he said, "patients won't be given paperwork to fill out at every appointment. Nurses won't have to spend time entering data into a computer or filing charts. A patient will walk into their appointment and give their name. The admitting nurse will confirm their information on the computer, and they'll be ushered into their appointment. Everyone who sees them will know why they are there. They'll know what they are going to do, and they'll know where the results will be sent." He could see the wonder in the eyes of several people. "And later that same day, the patient will have the results in their email inbox.

"We'll have better integration between all departments, more patient-centric focus, better work processes for everyone, and we also get an interface that provides for EHR exchange between hospitals and clinics so clinics and doctors with admitting privileges can send information directly to the hospital. When their patient arrives, we'll have all the information."

Gordon could see a light of understanding in the eyes of some of the people in the room. They were getting it.

"How long will this project take?" one of the board members asked.

"Six months until we're ready to go live, but probably nine months before we've got everyone comfortable with the system," Gordon said. "Which is why we need to get started now. With the onset of flu season in the fall, we want to make sure everyone is ready to go on the new system so there won't be hiccups when things get hectic."

"What do the nurses and doctors say? What if they aren't supportive?" asked another board member.

"That's exactly why we have a governance committee and why we will be forming a steering committee made up of key members from each department. They'll be kept abreast of the progress, as well as have responsibilities to see that the implementation goes well. They'll be able to act as a liaison for the project with their department so that everything gets communicated in a timely and accurate manner." Gordon watched several heads bob as they began to grasp the concepts.

"How much?" came a voice from the back. It was Myles Starkweather, the man who had started the largest office machine and technology company in the western US and who was currently the senior member on the board.

Gordon clicked to the slide with the budget and felt the mood of the room drop, as tangible as if someone had lowered the thermostat.

"Yes, this is a big project, and it will require a big budget," Gordon said. "But upgrading our HIS isn't an *IF* proposition. It's a *WHEN*. To give Grace hospital a competitive edge, to provide doctors, nurses, technicians, and others a technologically efficient place to work, with all the tools they need to provide the best care to our patients, now is the time."

The meeting came to an end and many of the attendants thanked Gordon for his presentation. Myles told him to expect an answer by the end of the week. Now all he could do was wait.

* * *

"He's driving me crazy," Tricia said. "I don't know how much longer I can do this. He said today that he refuses to drink any more water."

"How much are you giving him?" Gordon asked, trying not to smile. Tricia was clearly frustrated, but the thought of Jacob's powerplay being water refusal made him want to chuckle.

"The doctor said, *lots of water*, so I'm bringing him a glass every hour or so." She held up one of their bigger drinking glasses as an example. Poor kid.

"I bet he's had plenty of water," Gordon said kindly. "He's probably bored out of his mind." While Jacob recovered from his concussion, he'd had to sit in a darkened room and try not to think. No TV, no video games, no reading. Even music was supposed to be low volume and non-jarring, which was the exact opposite of what Jacob normally preferred to listen to. "I'll talk to him." He found his son lying on this bed, staring up at the ceiling as a white noise machine played the sound of ocean waves in the background.

"Hey, kiddo," Gordon said as he entered the room.

Jacob grunted. "Mom is driving me crazy," he said.

"Too much water?" Gordon guessed.

"I have to go to the bathroom, like, twice an hour," he complained. "Can't I be done resting? I want to play baseball again."

Gordon felt his son's pain. He couldn't imagine how difficult it would be having to not think for a few days. Sure, it sounded kind of nice in theory, but after thirty minutes, he knew he'd be ready to make a break for it. Still, when it came to his son, he didn't want to take chances. "Tomorrow is day seven, right? You just have to hang in there a little longer. You don't want to get injured again before you've fully recovered. It's best to wait."

Having to tell his son *no* was not lost on Gordon. Maybe this is how Myles and the rest of the board and executive team felt about the HIS project? Could it be that he was asking for something the hospital wasn't ready for?

"Can I at least go to the game this weekend?"

"I don't see why not," Gordon said, still distracted by his thoughts.

"Really?" Jacob said. "Mom said, *We'll see*, which means no."

"I'll talk to her." Gordon patted Jacob gently on his shoulder. "And maybe we can see about getting you thirty minutes of video games?" He quickly clarified when Jacob's eyes lit up, "Nothing crazy. Maybe Angry Birds."

His son nodded, agreeing. "Thanks, Dad," he said, and Gordon slipped from his room to talk to Tricia, hoping she would be easier to convince than Myles Starkweather.

Chapter 14
April 2010

Rain pelted the window of the conference room, the fluorescent lighting doing its best to dissipate the gray gloom that seeped in from outside, but none of that could dampen Gordon's spirit. "It's a go," he said as he dropped a stack of folders and his laptop on the table. Cheers and clapping erupted.

"Great job," Beau said.

"So, this is happening," Alberta said, a gleam in her eye. "Things are going to get crazy." She rubbed her hands together like she was warming up for a fight.

Gordon could always count on Alberta to say just what she was thinking. "As always," he chuckled, "my goal is to minimize the *crazy* and manage the change. First things first, though. We need to set up a steering committee."

"I don't understand," Phillip, the facilities manager, said. "We already have a governance committee. Isn't that enough?"

"The steering committee is project-specific. They'll be our boots-on-the-ground advocates from start to finish for the HIS project. That's why I'm going to need a subject matter expert, an SME, from every department. In fact, if you've got names now, let Fiona know and she'll reach out to them to organize our first meeting." Gordon plugged his laptop in to the projector and started setting up while Fiona quickly scribbled down names.

"Great," Gordon said, clicking through to the first screen. "This is a proposed timeline for the project. I need everyone's feedback before we get started because getting this project done on time will be critical. If we aren't finished by the start of flu season, things could get dicey as beds start filling up. Getting trained on a new system will take a back seat to caring for patients and that could derail a lot of our work."

"Remember what happened last year with H1N1," Alberta said with an eye roll.

"Don't remind me," Yumi threw back her head, rubbing her eyes. "We couldn't keep enough Tamiflu in stock for everyone who needed it. Phones rang off the hook and there was a constant line of people waiting to be seen for weeks."

"We barely had time to grab a drink of water, we were so busy," Alberta said.

"Right," Gordon added. "So, you can only imagine what will happen when we're trying to roll out a whole new system and don't have time to train or report and fix some of the issues that will undoubtedly pop up. We need to ensure that doesn't happen."

"The SMEs will need time to do configurations for the system," Fiona said. "They'll make sure the HIS has the elements each of their departments want. They'll be key in communicating to IT how they perceive their processes running."

"The SMEs will also be our departmental advocates for the changes that are coming and help people get past their fear of change," Gordon added. "As you can see, it's going to take a coordinated effort, but with the right organization and execution, this project will run smoothly."

* * *

Three months into the project things were going well, especially with the steering committee Fiona had taken leadership over. Gordon took a seat while she set up the projector and watched the SMEs from every department file in a full five minutes before the meeting was scheduled to start. According to Fiona, there was no *on time*. There was *early* or *late*, and if you weren't five minutes early, you were considered late. Gordon had to admire Fiona's communicating her expectations and holding people to them. She started with a status check.

"How is everyone doing with their departments?"

Brad, the SME for the physician's department, spoke first. "I'm getting pushback from some of the doctors," he said. "A few claim they are perfectly happy with the way things are and don't see any need to change."

"That's not good", Fiona said.

Gordon had seen this before. "By any chance have these doctors been here for a long time?" he asked.

Brad gave a sly grin. "How'd you guess? One in particular is saying his record-keeping methods have worked for years and that change is too much work."

"The more accurate, coordinated information you bring back to your departments, the better understanding everyone will have and the easier it will be to get them to buy in," Gordon explained. "Have you met with these doctors as a group or individually?"

"Both," Brad said. "And to be fair, most of the doctors are looking forward to the changes. They recognize that when we get this done, we'll be able to serve our patients better. We'll be faster, see more patients, and be more confident in our diagnosing and prescribing."

"That's what I'm hearing from the pharmacy, too," the pharmacy SME said.

"The nurses are cautiously optimistic," someone else chimed in. "But overall, they're looking forward to having more confidence in the accuracy of the data."

"Of course, we're going to encounter resistance to something this big," Fiona said. "It's going to require a lot of patience from everyone." She looked at Brad. "But with consistent communication and messaging, we should be able to work through most of that resistance."

Brad nodded reluctantly. "I'll keep trying," he said.

* * *

A few weeks later Gordon was going over the proposed IT budget in his office before his afternoon meeting with Meeta. He looked up as Fiona entered and when she didn't bother with a greeting, he knew something was up.

"We have a problem," she said. "Brad says Dr. Riley is refusing to use his iPad during patient appointments. A few other doctors who were on the fence about the new tech have decided since Riley's not using it, they don't have to either." She let out a long breath of frustration. "I've coached Brad through several scenarios, but he says Dr. Riley won't even talk with him about it anymore."

"Where's Beau? Does he know about this?" Gordon asked.

"It's possible. Brad's kept him updated on the situation. But he's on the east coast for a funeral and won't be back for three more days."

Gordon thought for a minute. Ideally, Beau would handle this situation. These doctors all reported to him, regardless of their seniority. But Dr. Riley's attitude was apparently spreading. They didn't have three days to wait for Beau to return. Gordon pushed back from his desk and stood. "Okay, come with me," he said.

"What are you going to do?"

"Well, I'll start off by listening."

Their timing was perfect because they found Doctor Riley in between patients, taking care of some paperwork in his office. He shelved his frustration and pasted on a smile he hoped looked genuine. "Hello, Doctor." Gordon kept his voice light. "Do you have a minute to talk?"

A smug look crossed the old man's face before he replied, "I think I know what this is about." The doctor's thick white hair matched the white coat hanging behind him from a hook on the wall. He gestured to the chairs on the other side of his desk.

"Well, then," Gordon started, "I won't beat around the bush. We just wanted to find out why you aren't using the iPad. We're working hard to implement this new system and I know it's a little hard making changes, but ultimately this will make things easier for everyone."

"You want to know what the problem is?" Doctor Riley said. "Let me introduce you to a simple phrase we used to say: *If it ain't broke, don't fix it*. And this isn't broke," he said, waving a pencil in the air.

Gordon kept quiet and let the doctor speak.

"You've got these fancy devices that are supposed to be *easier*." He gestured toward the white box peeking out beneath a stack of files. "But what happens when it doesn't turn on? What about when I tap that screen and nothing happens?" Dr. Riley's voice stayed even, but it was clear in his rigid delivery that a vein of tension ran just below the surface. "This right here," he said, waving his pencil through the air. "It's always on. If it gets dull, I sharpen it. That's it. Simple. You say that gadget is going to make things easier, but how much easier can you get than a pencil?"

"You make a great point." Hopefully finding common ground would lower his defenses a bit. "But a pencil creates notes that must be transcribed," Gordon said. "That takes time and errors can, and often do, happen."

Dr. Riley let out a dismissive puff of air. "I'll only be here for another year. Surely, they can put up with my old ways until then. Then you can do whatever you want, and I won't be here to complain about it."

"But everyone else will be moving on to the new HIS," Gordon countered. "You understand, for someone to stop and take your notes and go to the old system, which will be less accessible, or to create a paper record, just for your patients, will not only slow down those who have to do the work, but it will also slow down care for your patient as their records will be more difficult to locate. They won't be where everyone else's are."

"Like I said, it's just for a year." The doctor folded his arms across his chest as he leaned back in his chair.

Gordon didn't know what else he could say to convince the man to get with the program and he had to admit, the doctor's dismissiveness was making his blood pressure rise. Luckily, Fiona spoke up.

"Have you tried using the iPad?" she asked.

"I gave it a fair shot. Pain in the ass if you want to know the truth."

"What specifically was painful about the experience?" She spoke with the patience and sincerity Gordon was struggling to tap into.

"Everything about this thing is painful," he said. "First of all, it takes forever to turn on."

"That doesn't sound right, why don't you let me check it?" He passed the box to Fiona, and she removed the sleek tablet and pressed the power button. A moment later the screen lit up, the icons for the apps falling into place.

"It was giving me more trouble when I tried it," he said, a little sheepish. "And shutting it down and turning it back on between every patient, well, the extra wait time adds up."

"You know, you don't have to turn the tablet off every time you're done using it," Fiona said. "You can leave it on all day and shut it down at night."

"I wouldn't run down the battery?"

"You won't," Fiona said, then added, "The battery will last all day. No problem."

That seemed to interest Dr. Riley. "Well, it still won't ever beat a good ol' reliable pencil."

"Why don't you show me what's causing so many problems?" Gordon kept quiet and let her keep going because whatever she was doing, unlike him, Fiona seemed to be making progress.

The doctor took the tablet from Fiona and pressed the home button. The IT department had taken time to set up every iPad with the apps everyone would need, and to delete things they didn't, so it would be user-friendly. She watched as Dr. Riley tapped on the icon for the patient portal. Nothing happened. He tapped again. Still, the program didn't open. He quickly gave up and pushed the iPad across the desk. "You might as well just take it back. I can't use this thing."

Fiona tapped the screen and the app opened right up. "Hmm," she said as she took her own iPad and pulled a stylus from the holder in the case. "Why don't you try it with this?" She said and pushed the tablet back across the desk, holding out the stylus. "Just use it the way you'd use a pencil, except instead of writing, you're just going to tap."

Reluctantly, Dr. Riley took the stylus and gave the tablet another chance. When he tapped the patient portal with the stylus, it opened right up. "Well, that's just working now because you're sitting here," he said, the grumpy veneer thinning just enough to hear the humor in his voice.

"Go ahead and see if you can access patient records to add information." The doctor tapped a few more times with the stylus, successfully navigating to the correct screen. "Sometimes people with dry skin can't make the touch screen work," she said. "I'm guessing you have dry skin?"

"Extremely," he said. "I use enough hand cream that I should probably buy stock. This little tool makes a big difference."

"Why don't you keep that stylus," Fiona said. Then quickly added, "As long as you promise to give the iPad another chance."

He sighed, defeated and not yet ready to give in. "I'll give it one more week. If I don't find it easier by then, I'm out."

"Thanks, Doctor. And if you have any issues, please let me know and I'll be right over to help you," Fiona finished.

"Nicely done," Gordon said as they walked back to their department. "How did you know that thing about the dry skin?"

"We got my grandma an iPad for her birthday so she could read books, play sudoku, and FaceTime her grandkids. She had the same problem. Turns out it's a pretty common problem with older people. A stylus solves the problem, though."

"Huh." Gordon pondered this as they returned to their department—both the fact that she'd known about this, but also that she'd so sensitively worked it into the conversation.

"I'll talk to the nursing staff so they're aware of his concerns with the technology," Gordon said. "If they can help during rounds, and intervene before he gets frustrated, maybe we can get him on board."

"I was thinking the same thing," Fiona said as they reached the IT department.

Gordon took pride in her thought process. "So much of what we're doing is managing the change—trying to get our projects to have as little impact on daily work life for everyone." Gordon remembered many conversations with Tom about this same thing. "We do this by anticipating everything that could possibly go wrong and creating a contingency plan."

"That sounds like a lot of contingency plans," she said.

"That's the job," Gordon replied. "The more you can anticipate and plan for, the better the project will run, and the happier people will be." This was one of most valuable lessons he'd learned over his years in IT. "When everyone is happy, you build trust. Once you have the trust of your internal clients..."

Fiona cut him off. "Then you can focus on gaining the trust of your external clients," she finished.

"Oh, have I mentioned this before?" Gordon feigned offense but his laugh gave his light mood away.

"A few times," Fiona smiled. "And it's great advice. I'd honestly never thought of my responsibilities extending to vendors, but when you think about it, it makes sense."

Gordon paused as he returned to his office and wondered if this is what Tom had felt like when they'd worked together at Mama Meg's. Helping other people grow in their IT careers was entirely satisfying. If this is what being an IT consultant was like, he could see why Tom loved it.

Chapter 14

Six months later, the project neared its end. The only thing remaining was to go live, identify any problems, and quickly fix them. Gordon sat in on the steering committee meeting while Fiona received status updates.

"What's the report from the nurses?" she asked.

"Actually," Marci, the nursing SME said, "I'm hearing from a lot of nurses that they don't feel comfortable enough with their training to go live."

"I had a couple of doctors say the same thing," Brad said. "We did a few extra trainings and some of the doctors who felt more confident with the tech agreed to mentor those who were still unsure. You'll never guess who our biggest advocate and mentor is," he said, his smile incredulous. "Dr. Riley."

Fiona smiled as a few surprised reactions bounced around the room.

"I love your idea, Brad," Fiona said, bringing everyone's attention back to the meeting agenda, "would that work for you, Marci? Could we assign a buddy system to nurses so they know someone will be on hand to answer questions?"

"I'll run that past Alberta, but it seems like it should work." Marci scribbled a few notes on her meeting agenda as Fiona continued.

"I can't imagine it would be needed more than a few weeks to a month. I think everyone will be surprised that the learning curve for the tablets and ensuite computers will be very short."

"If Doctor Riley can learn, anyone can," someone said.

"Great point." Fiona turned to Gordon. "Do you have anything to add?"

"Thank you, yes," he said. "We're two weeks from going live. For the most part, we've stayed on schedule. Luckily, we worked a little extra time into the schedule for bumps in the road. But right now, we will need about one or two months to find out where the problems are and troubleshoot so that we will be ready for the increased hospital load when flu season hits. We've got to get everyone using the system and communicating any issues as soon as they crop up. Do you all have the right protocol for submitting work orders?" Gordon asked the room. "IT will be as efficient as possible in working through those. In fact, Fiona has a team dedicated to just that. We want to be as efficient as possible in order to minimize disruptions as we work through the first few weeks and months."

Everyone nodded and Gordon fielded a few questions about the work order protocol until everyone felt confident with the process.

"We appreciate your work in communicating all these things with your departments. You're a crucial link in the success of this project," Fiona said. "Our next meeting will be a week after we go live, and we'll talk more then."

* * *

Three months later

"Gordon, the numbers look great," Myles Starkweather said. "I know it's a little early, but so far, the board is thrilled with the direction the numbers are heading. Errors are down, which reduces our liability."

"I'm hearing that the nursing staff feels like they're able to give better care because they have all the information they need right at their fingertips when they walk in a patient's room. Same with doctors. Alberta says they're spending more time with patients, discussing their concerns rather than just dealing with the medical issues," said Gordon.

"That's one more thing that will drive up our star rating, which is always good news," Myles said. "I sit on the board for St. Vincent's, too, and will definitely share your success here with them. Don't be surprised if they want to have you do a presentation at one of the meetings."

"Thanks. It was a team effort for sure. A lot of moving parts. But I'd be happy to share what we learned," Gordon said, taking the chairman of the board's proffered hand.

"Well, you kept them all moving beautifully."

Epilogue
2015

Gordon found himself a quiet corner at the hotel bar and took a seat. He'd never heard of the two teams playing soccer on the bar TV, but he watched anyway. The bartender took his order and for the first time since that morning, Gordon relaxed. He'd told Tricia he'd call before he went to bed, but he still had an hour or two before that would happen. The goodnight call had become a tradition whenever Gordon traveled, and even though Tricia complained that he never had anything interesting to tell her, he knew she still liked to hear from him.

It had been a long day of conferences at the annual SIMposium, a three-day conference put on by the Society for Information Management. A stack of business cards from people who'd talked to him after his keynote address weighed down his coat pocket. While he loved making connections, he needed a break. The bartender had just brought his beer when he heard someone calling his name. *Couldn't he just have a few minutes to himself?* His initial dread turned to delight when he saw who it was.

"Nice job on the speech." Tom approached and clapped Gordon on the back. "I bet it feels good to be done."

"It does, but they've got me doing a workshop tomorrow, too."

"No rest for the weary," Tom chuckled as he took a seat next to Gordon and ordered an ale. "Your work at Grace is getting attention. I hear several other hospitals are following your lead."

Tom didn't do small talk. It was one of the things Gordon liked most about him. No matter how many months or years it had been since they'd last talked, he always just jumped right into the conversation. Gordon followed his lead. "The technology is inevitable. Every hospital will need to update eventually." Gordon took a drink of his beer. Man, that hit the spot.

"Yes, but it's not just adopting the technology; it's using your project organization techniques. That's what's unique."

"I learned from the best," he said and clinked his pint glass against Tom's.

"So, what's next at the hospital?" Tom asked.

"Honestly, things are running pretty smoothly. I'm in maintenance mode for the most part—going to meetings with the executive team and staying on top of the latest technology; looking for the next hospital project."

A look of understanding passed between them as Tom nodded. "That must be interesting."

"It is..." Gordon's words hung in the air, the sentence obviously unfinished. Tom must have sensed it because he waited for Gordon to continue. "But..."

"I knew there was a but coming," Tom smirked and took another drink.

"...I don't feel as challenged as I did when I was running the HIS project, or when I was reforming the IT department at

MedTech. Or even when we were updating the ERP at Mama Meg's. Those projects were exciting. I had to constantly be on my toes. Big problems came up and I didn't know how I would solve them. It was like a puzzle, and when I stepped back and applied all the principles that I'd learned—that you'd taught me all those years ago—the pieces eventually fell into place. It was a rush. Now, I don't quite know what to do with myself."

"I know the feeling well," Tom smiled.

"You do?" Gordon swiped a hand across his forehead. "Because I wondered if I was going crazy. Why can't I just relax when things are running well and enjoy my success? Tricia was actually starting to worry," he laughed.

"That's why I started consulting," Tom said. "I wanted to solve big problems. Run major projects. Not worry about the day-to-day workings of an IT department. Being a consultant allows me to do the part of the job I'm most passionate about."

Gordon rubbed the stubble on his chin. "That actually makes a lot of sense." He considered Fiona, who had stepped up in the last year and was ready for more challenges. Whether that was at Grace or somewhere else, Gordon couldn't say. But he did know that she'd make a great CIO one day if that's what she wanted to do.

"You're making quite a name for yourself, too," Tom pointed out, shoving the day's program across the bar. "Keynote *and* workshop presenter…that's the kind of thing that people notice," he said, before downing the last of his ale.

Gordon enjoyed his speaking engagements for the networking opportunities they provided. But the opportunity to teach and mentor someone else the principles of IT were what really excited him. It's why he'd booked as many conferences as his vacation time and Tricia would allow. "That's an interesting thought," he admitted. "Know of any openings anywhere?"

"Actually," Tom's eyes brightened, and he leaned forward on his stool. "My firm is working on signing a client who would be perfect for you. That is, if you were ready to take the next step in your career."

"Really?" Gordon's mind filled with the possibilities. He'd be lying if he said he hadn't thought of moving on from Grace, but up until now, in his mind, the path forward had always led to another CIO position. He'd been interviewed by several tech journals and was getting pinged multiple times a week through LinkedIn, so it wasn't like he didn't know about other opportunities. But nothing felt quite right. He had a strong background in manufacturing and healthcare and a decent background in education. That opened a lot of potential jobs. But he hadn't considered consulting until now.

Tom emptied his pint and set it back down on the bar. "You understand how IT contributes to the competitiveness of an organization," he said. "And you're great at communicating that to non-tech folks. You understand the IT pyramid and why it's important. You've always been a great business analyst. Plus, you're great with people. You'd be a natural."

"I like everything you're saying," Gordon said as he finished off his own drink. "And I think we should keep talking." Maybe his phone call with Tricia tonight would be interesting to her after all.

TOOLS & TIPS

The IT Value Pyramid

The "IT Value Pyramid" is a term coined to succinctly capture the three key roles of the Information Technology department and function in any organization. IT is an integrating function that glues together various information systems and diverse business processes to form the value chain for customers. It may help to think in terms of the three key and distinct roles of IT and how any IT department can work to perform them well. These are IT-as-Dial Tone provider (Service Provider), IT-as-a-Lever (Partner), and IT-as-a-Driver (Leader).

IT – Opportunities and Challenges

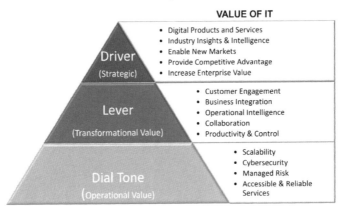

IT Value Pyramid

VALUE OF IT

Driver (Strategic)
- Digital Products and Services
- Industry Insights & Intelligence
- Enable New Markets
- Provide Competitive Advantage
- Increase Enterprise Value

Lever (Transformational Value)
- Customer Engagement
- Business Integration
- Operational Intelligence
- Collaboration
- Productivity & Control

Dial Tone (Operational Value)
- Scalability
- Cybersecurity
- Managed Risk
- Accessible & Reliable Services

A recent survey conducted by Deloitte and Wall Street Journal, found that 86% of U.S. CEOs say that technological advances will transform their business over the next five years. The Covid-19 pandemic clearly showed the overwhelming importance of technology in sustaining business and competing effectively in the long term. 67% of CEOs say IT is only somewhat prepared or not prepared to lead the changes needed. Clearly IT needs to up their game.

Some common observations regarding IT are:

- **CEOs Judge IT by the "Noise Level"**
    - o Quantity and tone of management feedback vs. value metrics
- **Line Management's Vision is Siloed**
    - o Focused on their own group/division/ department
- **IT Leader's Vision is Narrow**
    - o Focused on technology itself more than the business benefits
- **"No IT Involvement Required" is a Selling Point**
    - o What does this say about IT alignment and agility?

Ascending the IT Pyramid — from Dial Tone to Driver

The reality is that IT must start to make improvements at the bottom, foundational layer of the IT Pyramid before they are allowed to have meaningful conversations at the upper layers of the pyramid.

IT as Dial Tone

"Dial Tone" is defined as a service that provides easy, universal access using a variety of devices and regardless of location.

IT Dial Tone denotes:

- Readiness to provide service
- Assurance that service is available
- Any time, any place

The first step is for IT to be managed to provide "Dial Tone" type service to its customers.

IT as a Lever

A "Lever" is defined as a device that makes it easier to move large objects. Levers provide mechanical advantage, i.e., in business terms, great return on investment.

IT uses technology as a Lever to:

- Make business processes easier
- Get more from less
- Increase value of business services

The second step is for IT to partner with the business to become a great lever. The needed conversation for this step can only occur after the Dial Tone has been mastered.

IT as a Driver

A "Driver" is something that makes important things happen, for example, in an organization or economy.

Ultimately, IT Uses Technology to Drive:

- Creation of new products or services

- Opening of new markets

- Gaining competitive advantage

The Three Transformations

The current reality is that IT function must transform or it will become strategically irrelevant. Key reasons include that IT is not truly under central control, and cloud-based services are making it easy to source services externally without the IT department's involvement. Digital business and business transformation creates a great opportunity for IT leaders to lead transformation. To earn a seat at the table, IT leaders must become business experts, lead innovation, AND be successful at Dial Tone and Lever. Here is our view of the step-by-step transformation that IT must go through to improve its perception and value to the organization.

IT organizations may start at different points of the transformation:

1. IT does not work

2. Technology Focus

3. Internal Business Focus

4. External Business Focus

IT Value Meter

The goal of the transformation remains for IT to become externally business focused and a leader in the organization that can use technology to drive customer satisfaction, derive competitive advantage, and enable new digital products and services where none might have existed.

The Roadblocks

Common roadblocks in the transformation include:

- Stuck in the Day-to-Day (Tactical)
- Low Executive Support
  - o No Formal Company Strategy
  - o Cost Focus / Poor IT Brand
  - o Low Trust Environment
- Lack of CIO Skills
  - o Good Ideas / No One is Listening

IT leaders will be challenged to find a way to overcome these roadblocks and make progress. Sometimes outside coaching and mentoring can be leveraged.

The IT Pyramid – Skills Required

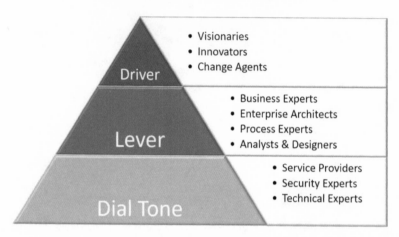

Each layer of the IT Value Pyramid requires certain distinct skills to become proficient. IT transformation requires that these skills be acquired and developed in order for IT to stay relevant. Skills required at every level include leadership, planning, product/service management, and change management.

Keys to Success

The IT leader can achieve success by leveraging the following strategies:

- Change The Conversation / Adapt your Persona

- Foster C-Suite Engagement & Participation

- Successfully Promote Systems Thinking

In conclusion, the IT Value Pyramid is a model used to explain the three key and distinct roles of IT in a business organization. Each upper layer can only be built upon a solid foundation of the previous layer. The model can be used for IT to understand its role in the business, deliver what is needed, and ultimately deliver great value to business and its customers.

TOOLS & TIPS

Changing the Conversation

Most IT leaders start their career in a technical IT role. As their career progresses, they improve their technical skills (technical diagnosis, design, implementation, etc.) substantially. However, to be an effective IT leader, they also need strong customer-facing skills including communication, empathy, and ability to build trust with customers. To learn the needed skills requires patience, diligence, and practice.

Your Value Vs. Your Perception

A good place to start is to consider your value proposition as an IT leader. A value proposition is a promise of value to be delivered, communicated, and acknowledged. It is also a belief from the customer about how value (benefit) will be delivered, experienced, and acquired.

Your Value vs. Your Perception

You may perceive your value to exist in any of the circles on the picture above. However, your sweet spot of best value will be found at the intersection of:

- What you know and can contribute
- What key stakeholders want and expect and believe
- Common business objectives

Six Sins in Business Conversations

Many business users think IT people speak a different language. This perception is likely validated by the many interactions business users of technology have had with helpdesk personnel and other expert IT people over time. The developing IT leader must be careful about existing perceptions of IT people and must demonstrate effective communication skills.

The following mistakes are common for IT people in conversations with their business peers:

1. Using technical jargon (unless it's THEIR business jargon)

     o Do not use IT terms in conversations with non-IT personnel. It is better to demonstrate mastery over business jargon to build better relationships.

2. Talking without listening

     o Practice active listening skills. Do not be thinking about a response while listening.

3. Interrupting while the other is talking

o   Demonstrate empathy while listening to non-IT people, especially when they are complaining about an IT problem. Take time to hear them out.

4.   Oversharing technical information

o   Avoid oversharing details of an IT solution or technical details. The users probably don't care about them.

5.   Acting inauthentic or unnatural in a conversation

o   Avoid feigning interest or strong disinterest in the conversation. Try to be natural.

6.   Remaining silent in the conversation

o   Practice active listening to have a real conversation

Adapt your Persona

A useful way to think about how to have the non-technical conversation with business users of technology is to think in terms of the IT Value Pyramid. Each layer of the pyramid in the figure below represents a different role for IT. As a member of the IT team providing IT services, be prepared to listen with empathy and work to improve service levels to meet service level agreements. As an IT Partner, be prepared to understand business challenges and design technology solutions to solve business problems. As a guide and leader, be prepared to lead the organization by demonstrating strong knowledge of markets and innovation in the organization's products and services through technology.

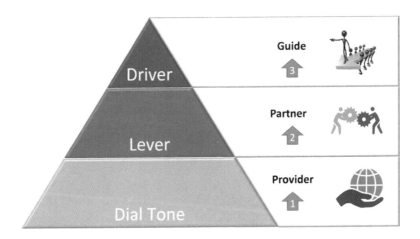

Challenge Exercise

Here is a practice exercise to change the conversation for a more successful outcome:

1. Pick a key person in your organization with whom communication has been a challenge

2. Prepare for your conversation as described above

3. Adopt a persona that you will use to match the audience and purpose of the communication

   o *Trusted Provider*: to address service concerns or issues

   o *Partner*: to help solve a business problem

   o *Guide*: to influence a management decision

   o Other as appropriate

Tools and Tips

Know Your Business

As a business leader and CIO, your goal is to enhance the value and operations of the organization where you work. In order to do that, you have to gather information about the organization's business environment:

- What does your company do?

- Who's the market leader in your industry & who's your major competition?

- What products are most valued by your customers (clients) & why?

- What is the next thing that needs to be done to make your company more competitive?

- How does IT contribute to the success of the company?

Get Involved with your Industry

The business environment almost always includes external organizations with ties to the particular industry segments. Typically, these external organizations are trade organizations that share common interests for their particular industry and hold regular meetings where topics of interest are discussed. The value of the trade organizations is that they share information that will allow a CIO to get information on regulatory issues, advances in technology, and unique applications of technology. They also provide the opportunity to interact with peers facing the same issues and problems. For example:

- Healthcare Information & Management Systems Society (HIMSS) provides CIOs information regarding issues and technology advances in the healthcare industry.

- Snacking-Nutrition & Convenience Intl (SNAC) provides information regarding snack foods.

- Brewers Association (BA) has information for craft brewers of beer.

- Credit Union National Association (CUNA) aggregates information from credit unions in the US and provides support in areas of regulatory compliance, new products available, and training.

- American Investment Council (AIC) works with investors, particularly in the area of private equity.

There are literally hundreds of these trade organizations available to help the CIO get a firm grip on what's happening in the industry and what the competition is doing.

Get involved with your company

Inside your company you need to find out what's going on and where technology can provide value and solve problems. So:

- Be Curious
    - o   What does your company do?

- o How does your company do it?
- o What are your peers' biggest headaches?
- o How can you help relieve those headaches?

- Be innovative. Show that IT can help solve problems in unique and innovative ways that provide your company with a competitive advantage.

- Be open and available. The most important thing you can do is to be there when you're needed. You need to build credibility and become a trusted advisor to your peers and their staff.

The 5whats-1how of IT

As a CIO you need to think about what you can do to help your organization achieve its mission and goals. By answering these questions and communicating with your peers and their staff you build the credibility of IT and become the 'go-to' team for all things technology related.

- What value does IT add to the company?
- Who can benefit the most from IT improvements?
- Where can IT improve business operations?
- When do you push and when do you pull back?
- Why is IT so important to the company?
- How can IT improve your company's competitiveness?

Six rules to live by

In short, do all of these things and your success as a CIO is assured.

- Get out of your comfort zone
- Understand your industry and how your company competes
- Get help – Find mentors and trusted advisors
- Hire smart – Find people who are more skilled than you are and lead them
- Know how your company runs - IT is involved in every aspect of the business
- Look ahead – If you're not thinking about next year, you're behind

Tools and Tips

IT Governance

Business Technology or IT Governance is a framework and set of accountabilities for making business decisions around technology across an enterprise. Effective IT governance is not just about making individual decisions, but includes well-defined roles and responsibilities, committees, budgeting processes, and decision-making processes that encourage behavior consistent with the organization's mission, strategy, and priorities.

IT Governance Objectives

Here are the key objectives of IT Governance:

1. Making the right investments to advance company strategic priorities

2. Clearly defining the business value of systems and ensuring investments are in line with return

3. Clearly identifying and managing project, technology, security, and compliance risks

4. Deploying the right resources to deliver and to sustain improvements

5. Measuring and demonstrating systems performance in terms of business value

Further, IT Governance is about:

- A portfolio of technology-driven business investments
- Prioritization (what's in/what's out/relative importance)
- Management oversight (services, performance, risks)

And IT Governance is NOT about:

- Adding bureaucracy
- Making daily/weekly decisions
- A proxy for IT leadership

Get started with IT Governance in your organization

IT has many facets and perceptions, and its business value can only be measured and interpreted by business executives. IT governance must be done by committee—usually called the IT steering committee. Take the following simple steps:

1. Form an IT steering committee consisting of key IT stakeholders.

2. Develop a simple charter for the IT steering committee including goals, expectations, membership, roles and responsibilities and mechanisms for risk assessment, increasing alignment, monitoring performance, and resource management.

3. Initially, have the committee meet monthly with an agenda to discuss key IT projects, assess progress, and take corrective actions where necessary. One committee goal should be to become tech savvy and learn how IT can be leveraged further for business.

4. Define an IT scorecard for the business. Perform a full annual evaluation of IT's contribution to the business.

This may sound like a lot of work. Some executives may think this is the task of the CIO or IT leader in their organization. This cannot be farther from the truth. Since IT has so many dimensions and affects almost everyone in an organization, IT governance cannot be undertaken solely by the IT leader.

Assessing IT governance maturity in your organization

As with any major change management effort, it can take years to implement changed business processes across organizations and get people to adopt new ways. Here is a simple way for organizations to know where they stand on the IT governance maturity scale:

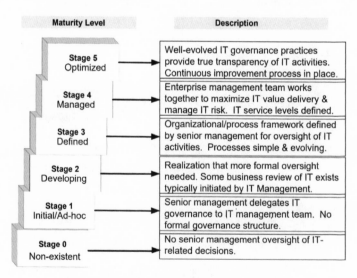

Maturity Level	Description
Stage 5 Optimized	Well-evolved IT governance practices provide true transparency of IT activities. Continuous improvement process in place.
Stage 4 Managed	Enterprise management team works together to maximize IT value delivery & manage IT risk. IT service levels defined.
Stage 3 Defined	Organizational/process framework defined by senior management for oversight of IT activities. Processes simple & evolving.
Stage 2 Developing	Realization that more formal oversight needed. Some business review of IT exists typically initiated by IT Management.
Stage 1 Initial/Ad-hoc	Senior management delegates IT governance to IT management team. No formal governance structure.
Stage 0 Non-existent	No senior management oversight of IT-related decisions.

(Adapted from ISACA COBIT Framework)

Most mid-size businesses starting out will find themselves to be at Stage 0 or 1. The key is to know where you stand and work on making progress to the next level which can take two to three years to implement.

When IT governance starts to work at any organization, many benefits are realized. First, business executives begin to make sense of the sometimes mysterious ways of IT. Second, they begin to work toward the good of the entire organization as opposed to optimizing only their part of the organization. Third, limited IT resources are allocated where they are most needed. Finally, regular monitoring of key IT initiatives uncovers problems promptly and ensures those problems will receive the attention they need from executives to get back on track.

For a more in-depth treatment of this topic, download our white paper titled "How to Align Information Technology with Your Business Needs" here: http://viellc.com/resources/

Key Success Factors

Here are some of the key success factors in the journey toward effective IT Governance:

1. Governance Board as appropriate for organization
2. Clearly articulated business values
3. Transparent management processes
   - o Planning: Goals are stated, shared and committed to
   - o Portfolio management of projects and services
   - o Risks are identified (without fear or blame) and managed
   - o Feedback loops in place

Tools and Tips

ITIL Overview

The Information Technology Infrastructure Library (ITIL) is a series of documents used to aid the implementation of a framework for IT Service Management. This customizable framework defines how Service Management is applied within an organization. Originally created by the UK government, ITIL is currently accepted as a standard for best practices.

ITIL consists of a series of books giving guidance on the provision of quality IT services, and on the accommodation and environmental facilities needed to support IT. ITIL has been developed in recognition of organizations' growing dependency on IT and embodies best practices for IT Service Management.

ITIL is organized into a series of sets, which themselves are divided into two main areas: service support and service delivery. Service support is the practice of those disciplines that enable IT Services to be provided effectively. Service delivery covers the management of the IT services themselves.

1. ITIL Service Support

Service Support is the area that enables IT Services to be provided effectively. The different Service Support disciplines are:

- Configuration Management

- Problem Management
- Change Management
- Help Desk
- Release Management

1.1 Configuration Management

Configuration Management involves setting up a central-ized database for provisioning and managing the IT services. Typically, this "Configuration Management Database" (CMDB) contains information relating to maintenance, asset manage-ment, and configuration.

Configuration Management consists of the following:

- Identification – the specification and identification of all IT components and their inclusion in the CMDB.

- Control – the management of each configuration item, specifying who is authorized to "change" it.

- Status – the recording of the status of all configu-ration items in the CMDB, and the maintenance of this information.

- Verification – reviews and audits to ensure the infor-mation contained in the CMDB is accurate.

1.2 Incident/Problem Management

Incident/Problem Management is the resolution and pre-vention of incidents that affect the normal running of IT services in an organization. This includes using a trouble ticketing system for tracking notification procedures, and periodic preventive maintenance.

1.3 Change Management

Change Management ensures all configuration or other operational changes are carried out in a planned manner. This includes authorized procedures, identifying the impact of each change, a backout procedure to reverse any changes, and a revision control system to keep track of older versions of configurations where possible.

1.4 Help Desk

The IT Service Help Desk is usually the first point of contact for all users when there is service failure or degradation. The Help Desk needs to be well informed by the engineers or operations staff of outages or planned downtime so that they can post this information for their users and should also have a way to escalate incoming issues to its more experienced and trained personnel.

1.5 Release Management

This is the management of configuration and versions of software within the organization. In addition to addressing the issue of several versions of the same software running within the organization, this also addresses the use of unlicensed and illegal copies of software.

There are several best practices in this area such as:

- creating a centralized software library
- controlled distribution and tracking licenses
- testbed or lab area for evaluating new versions before putting them into production

2. ITIL Service Delivery

Service Delivery is the management of the IT services themselves and involves a number of management practices to ensure that IT services are provided as agreed between the Service Provider and the Customer.

ITIL Service Delivery consists of five disciplines:

- Service Level Management
- Capacity Management
- Continuity Management
- Availability Management
- Financial Management

2.1 Service Level Management (SLM)

Service Level Management is the primary management of IT services, ensuring that agreed services are delivered when and where they are supposed to be delivered. The core of SLM is the service catalog which defines what services IT provides, under what conditions, and to whom. The Service Level Manager is dependent upon all the other areas of Service Delivery providing the necessary support that ensures the agreed services are provided in a secure, efficient, and cost-effective manner. Service level agreements are a critical component of SLM.

In order to measure SLM in IT networks, it is important to have a fault management system that can provide metrics such as downtime and availability reports.

2.2 Capacity Management

Capacity Management ensures that IT infrastructure is being utilized efficiently and it is available when needed at the right price. This requires:

- Performance monitoring
- Trend analysis for resource forecasting
- Application sizing

2.3 Continuity Management

Continuity Management (or Disaster Recovery) is the planning required to ensure that IT Services can recover and continue should a serious incident occur. In addition to reactive measures, it uses proactive planning to reduce the risk of a disaster. Business Continuity Planning (BCP) tries to extend the practice to ensure that the entire business process can continue in the event of an outage.

Continuity management involves the following basic steps:

- Prioritizing the businesses impacted
- Performing a risk assessment for the IT services
- Creating a disaster recovery procedure

2.4 Availability Management

Availability Management involves measuring and quantifying the service uptime or availability of business or IT services. These metrics are typically critical for defining Service Level Agreements:

- Availability (or uptime) percentage

- Mean Time to Recovery (MTTR) and Mean Time Between Failures (MTBF)

- Scheduled vs. un-scheduled downtime

- Help Desk statistics (number of calls, response times, resolution times)

2.5 Financial Management

IT Financial Management is reviewing the cost of the IT infrastructure including maintenance, ongoing cost of ownership, failures, replacement, etc. The costs include software, hardware, staff, training, replacement, etc.

Tools and Tips

Strategic Project Management

Project management has two essential components:

- Organization
- Risk Management

These components go together hand in glove to help ensure the success of any project that the organization undertakes, be it an IT project or any another project.

Project Management Organization

It is important to set up a structure that ensures project progress is reported to executive management on a timely basis. That structure consists of three layers:

1. The Executive Management Oversight Team
2. The Project Steering Team
3. The Project Implementation Team

Each of these groups has a specific function in the success of a project.

The Executive Management Oversight Team, sometimes called the IT Steering Committee, is responsible for coordinating and prioritizing all IT-related projects company-wide. This group is typically comprised of the executive management team, including the CIO. They typically invite Project Steering Team leaders to provide the current status of projects underway. This team meets on a regular schedule, typically bimonthly or quarterly, depending on the number and duration of projects that have been authorized. The meetings of this group can be contentious since each member of the management team has their agenda that they would like to see advanced. This is also a good forum for sorting out the relative strategic value of the projects under consideration. It almost becomes a review of the strategy and company goals.

The Project Steering Team sets project direction, allocates resources, monitors progress, and oversees the project budget. This group consists of the leaders of all the stakeholder departments affected by the project as well as the executive sponsor and the project manager. This team meets regularly on a monthly basis. They may meet more often if there are contentious issues that are unable to be resolved by the Project Implementation Team. There will be a project steering team for every major project in the company. If resource or progress issues surface at this level, this team will resolve them if they can. If the issues are related to other projects or affect the business strategy, they may be referred to the Executive Management Oversight Team. This team has the primary responsibility for delivering a successful project on time and within budget.

The Project Implementation Team is where the rubber meets the road. This team is responsible for developing and managing the project plan that will meet the project objectives. The team consists of the project manager, direct stakeholders, and subject matter experts as needed. The project manager is the interface back to the Project Steering Team. This team typically meets weekly to discuss cross-departmental business requirements, prioritize implementation tasks, test system functionality, and train other users. These individuals are responsible for communication with their departments. They have the most to gain from a successful project. Their departments will run better, their jobs will be easier, and they will be more productive if the project succeeds.

To recap, a good project management structure consists of three tiers:

IT Steering Committee

Role:	Strategy, Project Prioritization, and Funding
Members:	Executive Staff and CIO

Project Steering Team

Role:	Direction Setting
	Resource Allocation
	Progress Monitoring
	Budget Management
	Issue Resolution
Members:	Project sponsor (preferably an executive staff member)
	Project manager
	Key management stakeholders
	CIO (major projects)

Project Implementation Team

Role	Definition of functional requirements
	Recommendations on direction and vendors
	Implementation planning
	Issue Resolution
	Testing
	Acceptance
	Execution
	Post Project review
Members	Project Manager
	Subject matter experts
	Technology experts
	Key stakeholders

NOTE: Depending on the project size and scope, the Project Steering Team and the Project Implementation Team can be combined to eliminate duplication and make more efficient use of resources.

Project Risk Management

Every project has some level of associated risk. Historically, studies have shown a variety of factors contribute significantly to project failure

- Lack of user involvement
- Poor (or lack of) project planning
- Poor communication
- Rewarding the wrong actions
- Scope creep

- Naïve adoption of new technologies
- Too many people
- Too much reliance on
    - o Project management software
    - o Project methodologies

When projects are proposed they often suffer from the Seven Deadly Project Sins:

- Mistaking half-baked ideas for viable projects
- Dictating unrealistic project schedules
- Assigning under-skilled project managers to high-complexity projects
- Not ensuring solid business sponsorship (see Project Management Organization)
- Failing to break projects into manageable "chunks"
- Failing to institute a robust project process architecture
- Not establishing a comprehensive project portfolio to track progress of ongoing projects

For example, consider that a project has goals and objectives, faces risks, and must successfully manage the risks to deliver against the goals and objectives.

This leads to a straightforward approach to planning and managing projects by defining the risks facing a project such as exposures and obstacles, impacts of those risks, and the likelihood that those risks will arise. To manage the risk, you need to develop a risk management plan that includes mitigation and contingencies. You must proactively manage the project's risks.

Every project faces a combination of risks including:

- Requirements
- Resources
- Technology
- Political

- Schedule
- Budget/cash flow
- Competitive

Clearly, many activities are required to manage all of these risks. Ultimately, a project's risks determine its:

- Feasibility
- Resource requirements
- Probability of success

- Schedule
- Costs
- Delivery against goals and objectives

A common mistake is to assess risks too late in the project. Typically, a work breakdown structure (WBS) is constructed, then time estimates are prepared, resource requirements are assessed, budget and cash flows are baselined. Notice that risk assessment isn't included. Risk assessment should be an early activity in the WBS before other project tasks are initiated. This will provide a basis for a "go-no go" decision before significant resources are committed to the project.

Given that project risk can adversely impact a project, what is a project manager to do? Develop a comprehensive risk strategy as the first stage in project planning. Then develop a tactical risk management plan that implements the risk management strategy and is directly incorporated into the project plan.

Risk responses should be classified as follows:

- Avoidance
- Transference
- Retaining
- Mitigation
- Sharing

Where possible, you will want to plan actions by defining how those risks can be eliminated or mitigated. These actions may include:

- Risk-specific tasks
- Insurance policies
- Stage-gate analysis
- Acquiring specialized resources
- Project compression
- Quality assurance

Some risks must be addressed through contingency plans. It may be that the impact/probability of risk doesn't warrant up front action. Conditional actions (e.g., if event occurs, then perform specified tasks) may be adequate:

- Using secondary suppliers for necessary supplies, equipment, etc.
- Tasks to be performed only if something happens (e.g., tasks that must be performed if the project is disrupted by a strike)

The key is to establish these contingency plans up front, enabling a rapid response by the project team.

Assessing risk consists of the following activities:

- Identifying specific risks (e.g., necessary technologies cannot be integrated)
- Identifying undesirable events/trigger events

- Quantifying (where possible) the impact of each occurrence
- Determining the likelihood of occurrence
- Known, or inferred, probability distribution
- Subjective probabilities
- Distribution of time to event (if possible)
- Determining the likelihood of detection

Estimating impact magnitude and probability is critical because it's necessary for identifying which risks are worth addressing, it enables calculation of expected impact of each risk (e.g., what this risk can be expected to cost), and it provides the necessary foundation for developing a cost-effective risk management plan.

Essentially, a project manager's principal role is risk manager. That role is extremely challenging given the broad range of risks faced by most projects. It's easy to neglect when you focus on the project process/methodology and rely too heavily on project planning tools. Risks must be understood and accepted by the organization and project team.

In the end, making sure that everyone from executive management to the project implementation team are aware of the progress and risks of the project is the key to successful project management.

For an in-depth discussion of project risk management, see "Project Management: A Risk-Management Approach" by Ted Klastorin and Gary Mitchell.

Tools and Tips

IT Strategic Approach

Taking a strategic approach to Information Technology planning and implementation is critical for an IT leader to avoid waste both in the business as well as IT systems and processes. A strategic approach entails systemic thinking, understanding business direction, creating a matching IT strategy, strategic planning, and implementing plans over time through effective project management techniques.

Promote Systems Thinking

It is natural for people and even departments to be siloed in focusing on work and progress in their particular area or department.

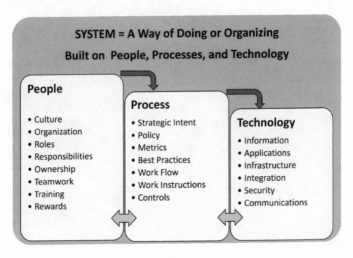

However, since any organization is a system, all the parts of an organization work together in a set of value chains that ultimately deliver value to the customer as promised by the brand. Information is a critical asset in any organization that integrates and ties various functions together to enable the smooth flow of value. Therefore, the IT department has a critical role in promoting systemic thinking across the organization. A good way to think about the system is that it is "A way of doing and organizing built on people, process, and technology." Since the IT leader is responsible for all the information systems, they have a critical role in promoting the adoption of systemic thinking across the organization.

What is your business strategy?

Some business organizations have a written business strategy. Many mid-size and smaller organizations do not have a written business strategy, but one that constantly evolves in response to external forces and business conditions. If the organization does not have an explicit written strategy, a critical part of the IT leaders' role is to discover and infer the strategy through interviews of key business executives. Here are some of the questions that should be posed in the discovery process:

- Executive Interviews
    o What has made the company successful?
    o What differentiates our business?
    o What is your vision for the organization in 3-5 years?
    o What needs to happen to realize this vision?

- Alignment
  - Where are the visions aligned? Where do they differ?
- External Forces
  - Competitors
- SWOT analysis

At the end of the day, IT exists to support the business. Therefore, a good understanding of the business direction and strategy is essential to build a strategy of the right IT investments over time.

The IT leader has one other critical leadership role in building business strategy: assessing the impact of new and emerging technology on existing business processes and on the potential for new digital products and services. With their intrinsic knowledge of emerging technology, the IT leader is uniquely positioned to advise the business on these key aspects.

Creating your IT strategy

An IT strategic approach consists of three layers of planning as shown:

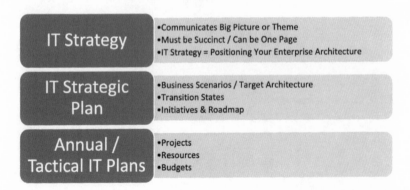

IT Strategy	•Communicates Big Picture or Theme •Must be Succinct / Can be One Page •IT Strategy = Positioning Your Enterprise Architecture
IT Strategic Plan	•Business Scenarios / Target Architecture •Transition States •Initiatives & Roadmap
Annual / Tactical IT Plans	•Projects •Resources •Budgets

It is best to take a top-down approach to building an effective IT strategy. It also helps to have a succinct description of the strategy on a single page for effective communication.

Here is an example of a one-page IT strategy:

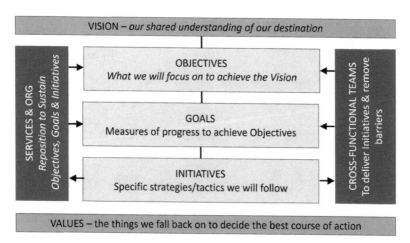

This tool can be used to communicate the direction, goals and high-level plans for IT in an easytounderstand manner.

IT Strategic Plan

Here are the suggested components of an IT Strategic plan:

- Executive Summary
- Company Vision, Goals, Objectives, and Strategy
- IT Strategy
    - o Vision/Values/Principles
    - o Key Strategies
    - o Objectives/Goals/Initiatives/Measures
    - o Skills, Organization, and Sourcing

- Target Architecture
    - o Business Architecture
    - o IT Architecture (Information/Application/ Infrastructure)
- Roadmap
    - o Sequence/Timing to Implement Strategy

Communicating your IT Strategy

The final step in building an IT strategy is communicating it in various forms throughout the business organization. Since IT is a pervasive function, the more users know about planned changes, the easier it will be to implement IT projects.

Here is a suggested outline of the communication:

- Why are we doing this? (tied to business needs)
- What are we doing? (what needs to change?)
- So that these business outcomes are achieved? (tied to business metrics)
- How will we do this?
- Who is affected by the changes?

Tools and Tips

Managing Information Technology

As an IT leader you have to consider IT's function within your organization by asking yourself the following questions.

- What is the central goal of IT?

- Is IT a service organization or a business growth contributor?

- Why are the bulk of IT resources typically focused on infrastructure management?

- Is it about the Technology or the application of the Technology?

- How should IT be organized to provide the greatest business benefit?

CIO Leaders Must Lead, Not Just Manage

Executive Leadership is founded on building and maintaining credibility. Leadership and management are not the same. CIO leaders need to do both. Leading is about change and influencing others to change. You must lead with your business colleagues to set expectations and to identify what is valued — the CIO's demand side. Second, you must lead your IT team to deliver on that; that is, to provide cost-effective services — the supply side of the CIO's role.

On the demand side, CIOs need to create a vision for how IT will both stimulate and support better business strategy for your company or agency. This means understanding the fundamentals of your environment, your industry, and engaging key stakeholders. Shape and manage informed expectations of your executive colleagues through identifying key business needs and articulating these as business maxims, then identifying the IT maxims that they require. Good governance is essential to effective collaboration amongst executives to weave together business and IT strategy.

On the supply side, CIOs need to build a lean and focused IT organization, a strong IT leadership team, refocus on process-based work, and a strategic sourcing process.

To bring it all together, you need to communicate your vision, your success, and your performance to others and help key C-level executives articulate the value of IT to the market.

Demand Side	Supply Side
Lead with your business colleagues by knowing what is valued	**Lead your IT team**
• Create and communicate an enterprise IT-enabled vision • Shape and manage informed expectations • Use good governance to weave business and IT strategy together	• Deliver cost-effective services • Build a lean and focused IT organization • Develop and nurture your team • Communicate IT-enabled performance

The Credible CIO Is the Basis of the CIO Leader

Many CIOs are somewhat confused about where their credibility comes from. Credibility comes from one thing: delivering results that your enterprise leadership cares about. Credibility is the result of an ongoing process that feeds itself. The CIO who is new is given initial credibility. Based on that credibility, the new CIO receives resources and permission to undertake IT initiatives. Those initiatives have outcome and results, which depend on what they are and the extent to which they benefit the enterprise. In the eyes of the enterprise leaders, they either enhance or diminish the CIO's credibility. The process becomes either a virtuous cycle or a downward spiral. Every success builds more credibility; every failure chips away at the CIO's credibility. Credibility requires building strong personal relationships. It means being politically smart, integrating IT objectives with enterprise objectives, and anticipating business needs to deploy a predictable stream of technology that enables business solutions.

To a large extent, leadership is built on the complex task of building and maintaining credibility. Credibility is truly the most basic asset needed by a CIO leader. And this asset is just one aspect of how leadership and management are different.

CIOs Must Earn Their Executive Leadership Position Through Influence and Outcomes

Leadership is about change and influencing others to change. Doing things differently requires vision, strategy, inspiration, and passion. As Heifetz in his Adaptive Leadership Principles says, "leaders are those who foster adaptive change, which requires people to alter their habits, ways of acting, and sometimes the way they think and feel." Change encounters resistance. Management on the other hand is about technical change. It involves improvement, doing something better or faster, rather than doing something new and different. Management is about execution, particularly planning, organizing, control, and analysis.

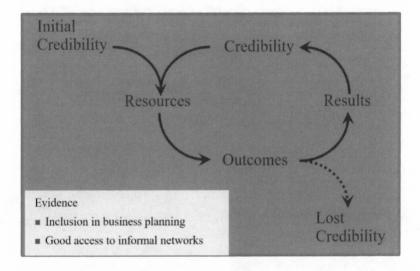

Joe Locandro from Yallourn Energy explains that management is about "What did you do today?" But "Leadership brings people forward on a journey by focusing on outcomes and directions. It says 'Come along with me.'" Both are necessary for success.

CIOs are generally strong on management, but often less strong on leadership. It's the leadership skills they need to strengthen, and such skills can be developed in anyone willing to work at it.

Leaders foster *adaptive* change, not just *technical* change. It's about altering habits, ways of thinking, leaving the familiar behind to focus on what the future looks like when those changes are made.

Leadership is about visioning, communicating. The "vision thing" is well articulated and relevant to the business. It provides a clear and compelling point of view that is simple, targets communications that are focused on recipient, and takes the time to communicate clearly.

- Leadership is about building relationships:

- Understanding and working within the political context

- Knowing your colleagues as people

- Developing your emotional intelligence so you can empathize with whomever you are communicating

The Demand and Supply Sides Build On, Continually Reinforce Each Other

CIO Leaders are IT executives who wish to become leaders in the face of the changing role of information technology. They are not content with the status quo. CIO leaders develop their agenda and deliver results that make an impact on their enterprise. CIO leaders know the importance of leading and managing both the demand and supply side of their jobs. Most often, though, they put a lot of their personal energy and relationship building efforts into the demand side — that is the part that only they can do. And they develop a strong team who will work with them on the supply side. This is critical because, recalling the Credibility Cycle, you don't get the recognition as a leading enterprise executive without being able to "deliver, deliver, deliver" and being perceived to do so by your executive colleagues.

Being a CIO leader involves focusing on the ten priorities outlined above. You won't give them all the same weight at the same time, but each of them is critical to earning genuine credibility as a valued executive colleague.

Tools and Tips

Technology as a Driver

Digital Disruptors

Over the last three decades, there have been a broad range of changes that have disrupted the way business operates. The vast majority of those changes are due to the introduction of digital innovations that have impacted business operations on all levels. Consider the timeline of digital advances. Each of these advances has altered the landscape of business and driven organizations to rethink how they interact with their customers and suppliers as well as how they conduct their business.

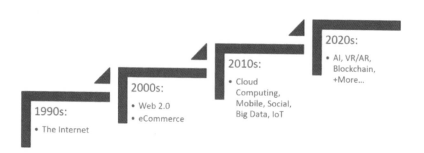

Digital Transformation

Digital Transformation is a term that describes what is happening to businesses and how they are adapting their business organization, processes, and customer relationships to meet the needs of a fast-changing digitally enabled business environment.

This new environment is forcing companies to innovate more rapidly and respond almost in real-time to shifts in customer demands. There are multiple impacts on business that can be categorized in three broad areas.

1. **The Rate of Change is outstripping the ability of business to keep up:** This is forcing businesses to develop new operating cultures that proactively adapt and continuously evolve. This means achieving business suppleness that is comprised of operational and strategic agility — where a business senses and responds to the customer needs quickly and continuously is key to the success. Past processes and approaches around establishing long-term strategies, annual budget cycles, annual talent management, and bureaucratic operational processes don't work in the digital world.

2. **Customers want what they want, when and where they want it:** Customers in a digital world have choices and preferences evolve. Successful businesses have learned how to develop deeper empathy with customers and delight customers across every touch point from initial interaction, to developing, delivering, servicing. and repeat use of their solution that satisfies their customer's needs.

3. **The Culture of business must embrace digital — top to bottom:** There are significantly different leadership mindsets and cultural behavior expectations for leaders to transform themselves and to be role models and change agents in an increasingly digital world. This has driven different leadership demands where technology is expected to bring various company functions together — it breaks down the traditional silos, enhances strategic alignment, re-engineers business processes, transforms culture, and provides the rich soil for growing the talent needed for business co-creation.

What happens if you play the ostrich and ignore this vast change that is occurring in business? With the rising pace of change, more businesses are getting disrupted more than ever before and experiencing a shorter life span. Businesses in the digital world are expected to create operating conditions where they are ready for continual evolution and proactively adapt as part of their new DNA or face extinction. And that is at the heart of any digital business transformation — businesses that successfully pursue digital business transformation agendas focus heavily on cultural change agendas and operate differently than their competitors.

As you can see from this chart, the lifespan of companies on the S&P 500 has been cut by half in last 30 years and at the current rate, 75% of the companies now on the S&P 500 will be removed in the next 10 years. Ignoring this change in business can be detrimental to your business' health.

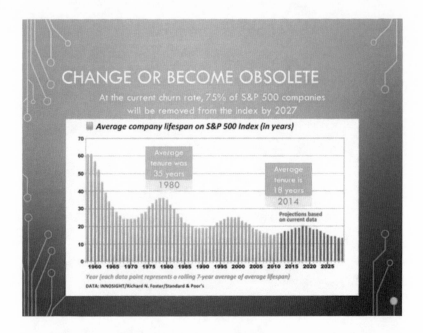

As a CIO, one of your responsibilities is to ensure the success of your organization through the application of evolving technology. The CIO is no longer just the keeper and maintainer of technology. The CIO must be aware of the emerging technology trends and understand how those trends will impact their organization and its operation.

Legacy vs. Emerging Role of the CIO

Legacy Role	Emerging Role
Department head who takes care of all our technology	Integrator who helps us adopt the right technology quickly
Takes orders and delivers what "the business" demands	Integral part of the executive team who guides our technology direction

Manages IT as a cost center. No value measures for information technology	Manages IT investments with a clear idea of the external value created
Business Units and IT buy stuff independently then worry later about how it all fits together	IT sets standards and partners internally & externally so that all services work in unison
Too busy keeping the lights on to think about innovation	Focused on helping our business win in the marketplace

Remember, the peak of the IT Pyramid is about technology as a driver. This is not about the technology itself, but rather the application of the technology to new ways of doing business, and providing value to the organization in the form of new services, products, and business operations in a way that provides a competitive advantage.

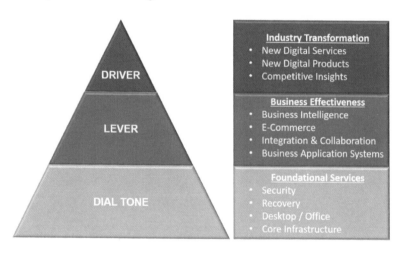

As a CIO you must answer these questions:

- What technology forces will disrupt your industry?
- Are these Threats or Opportunities?

- What can you do as an IT leader to prepare?

When you answer these questions, you will be truly using technology as a driver to grow and establish your organization as an industry leader.

Tools and Tips

Societal Impacts of Technology

Over the millennia, technology has immensely aided and impacted humans. We have progressed from living in caves, being hunters and gatherers, settling down in small groups employed chiefly in farming activities, and ultimately building megacities and nations to live in and prosper. Technology has always played a key role in these advances. The advent of computers and computing in the 1960s further impacted society and accelerated changes in ways that we are still trying to fully understand. With the arrival of Artificial Intelligence and "smart devices" in the 21st century, it is hard to envision the true impact on society over the rest of this century.

Over the last few decades many futurists have attempted to predict the future impact of technology on society. In an HBR article in May 2003, Nick Carr said that "IT doesn't matter" anymore. He predicted that Information Technology was quickly becoming a commodity and the business opportunity for gaining competitive advantage was quickly dwindling. He advocated spending less on IT both to reduce costs and reduce the risk of buying equipment that would become obsolete quickly. We think he was partially right.

Ray Kurtzweil, Director of Engineering at Google, predicts that the Singularity will occur by 2045. The singularity is that point in time when all the advances in technology, particularly in artificial intelligence (AI), will lead to machines that are smarter than human beings. So, is this really possible? What implications does this have on society in general and on jobs of the future? Will computers and robots have all the jobs after 2045?

In their book The Second Machine Age, Erik Brynjolfsson and Andrew McAfee say that the most influential development in history was the Industrial Revolution. We are now currently living through a second, comparable revolution that is changing how people use their minds to perform conceptual labor. Digital technologies are very important, and they're making our lives much better. The Internet is a huge part of this because it gives us access to information from all over the world. However, with great power comes great responsibility, and we must be careful not to let technology take control over our lives or make us lazy.

Current Impact of Technology

We lean on technology every day, and our expectations and demands of technology continue to grow. However, as with any tool, the way in which we use technology will indicate whether its effects are useful or harmful for society. Already we are seeing a series of positive and negative impacts.

1. Positive impacts of technology on society:

Technology has eased many onerous tasks in our daily routine and made living our lives much easier.

The following are some of the more positive aspects:

Improved Healthcare

As evidenced by the increasing life of the average adult, healthcare technology has helped humans tremendously over the last 100 years and continues to do so. Technology improvements include simple devices such as thermometers, blood pressure machines, diabetes monitors, various imaging techniques, laparoscopic surgery, patient information systems, and many others.

Improved Communication

We have progressed from letters that used to take weeks to arrive to the Internet which provides instantaneous communications around the globe with the use of a smart phone. Keeping in touch with other humans has never been easier.

Personal Productivity Enhancements

Our lives have become much easier with instantaneous access to information on the Internet to guide actions. Airplanes have made it possible to travel around the planet in less than a day. Other personal productivity improvements include general purpose computers with calendars and email, collaboration, task management, information sharing, and better overall work-life balance.

Improved Education and Learning Process

Access to learning and education is key to advancing careers. Technology enhances the education and learning process. Nowadays people can easily enhance their knowledge using the internet. Much of the data present on the internet is free of cost and you can access this data anytime and anywhere.

2. Negative impacts of technology on society:

One the other hand, a tool can also be misused. Here are some of more negative impacts on our society:

Increase in Health and Mental Concerns

Technology is affecting the physical as well as mental health of human beings. It makes people lazy, emotionally weak, induces sleeping problems, reduces physical activity, and can cause people to spend less time with their family and friends.

Unemployment

With machines taking over many blue-collar jobs, many people are finding it hard to retrain for newer technology-oriented jobs. They may be out of options, and many have given up looking for a job.

Long Term Climate Changes

Factory production processes produce toxic gases and other chemicals as a side effect. If not dealt with effectively, this has the potential to cause long term changes in our environment that could affect our long-term survival.

Cybercrime

Due to the excessive use of the Internet and lack of proper security controls, cybercrimes have increased. Many users are now at risk of extortion and having their digital identities stolen by attackers.

The Future of Computing and AI

Gordon Moore was one of the founders of Intel. In 1965, he famously predicted that the number of transistors on a chip would double roughly every 18 months without increasing costs. Since 1965, there have been periods of time when experts predicted that Moore's law will come to an end, but so far, it has not. It appears that Moore's Law will continue to deliver faster and cheaper computers well into the 21st century. The smartphone of today is similar in power to a supercomputer of the 1980s and 1990s. We do not expect Moore's law to stop delivering any time soon. This technology trend has strong implications for computing and networking for this century.

Narrow Artificial Intelligence is that which is programmed to solve a specific problem or perform a single task such as playing chess or composing music and cannot be used to perform any other task easily. As computing power gets cheaper and improves substantially, Narrow AI will get better, faster, and cheaper. One example of this is the much better quality personal assistants such Google Assistant and Apple's Siri programs. Narrow AI is very useful in many applications including personal productivity, health care, and computer vision. It will continue to improve our lives into the future.

General Purpose AI refers to machines that display human intelligence. This sort of intelligence would be able to enable robots to act like humans so that they are conscious, sentient, and driven by abstract thinking, emotion, and self-awareness. Sentience is hard to replicate in machines. We are not sure this type of computing can ever be achieved or even modeled.

The Future of Work and Income

Throughout history, the work done by humans has been transformed by work done by machines. Early examples include replacement of humans and animals in farming by tractors and other machines. Factories and tools on assembly lines worked by humans with specialized skills replaced humans who did most of the tasks manually. More recently, industrial robots have taken over more and more automation of factory work that was done by humans just a few decades ago. So, what is the future of human work?

In the early waves of automation, blue collar work was being automated and performed by machines. In the recent past, increasingly, white collar work is being performed by smart machines. Examples include writing articles, composing music, and medical diagnosis.

Many experts argue that there will always be work for humans as societies evolve and new categories of higher-level work are created. However, given the speed of innovation, and how fast new technologies are being adopted in the workplace, it is not clear that there will be sufficient work available in many people's current lifetimes.

Income Spread and Winner-Takes-All Reality in the Information Age

Digital technologies and digitization of work that used to be done by humans has had a deep impact on how work is shared between humans and computers. Innovation with digital technologies to convert old ways of doing work into new ways of doing work with computers is now a key predictor of how and where the income is shifting. An innovator who invents a slightly better and productive approach to an old problem can duplicate their solution and make it available to millions of customers at essentially zero cost. A large part of the economic benefit will flow to the inventor and their co-workers since it does not take many workers to produce such a solution. However, this solution may eventually put thousands of other humans out of work as the new solution is adopted by millions of users. A good example is that of tax software. Companies like H&R Block and Intuit are getting millions of dollars in software fees, while thousands of tax preparers may be losing their jobs.

In the age of digital technologies and computers, there will be a greater income gap and many workers will find themselves moving slowly toward the bottom of the spread while a few winners get extremely wealthy.

The consensus among futurists and economists about the future of jobs says that as a society we need to make the right investments in infrastructure, such as making the Internet truly accessible to all tiers of society. In addition, we need to increase focus on education to prepare our children and young and older workers alike to work and innovate in the age of new digital technologies. Governments may need to kick in with a minimum income guarantee to ensure a more equitable distribution of income to counter the increasing gap in income levels.

Your role as a technology leader in your organization is to ensure that the technology deployed at your workplace is used effectively to further the goals and mission of the organization. However, you also have a role in society as a whole to envision the impacts of technology and to advocate for mitigating solutions for those members of society who are negatively affected by the changes technology brings about.

Author Bios

Mike Scheuerman is a CIO Consultant for Virtual Information Executives. He brings over forty years of senior executive leadership skills and technical expertise with domestic and international operations to VIE's clients. He has worked in multiple industries, including financial services, health care, high tech manufacturing and higher education. Mike's Information Technology experience covers a broad array of skills, including Outsourcing Management, Customer Relationship Management, Supply Chain Management, Business Intelligence and Infrastructure Management. He is noted for creating strategic business and technology plans that drive significant growth while also focusing on cost containment.

Manoj Garg is the Founder and Managing Partner of Virtual Information Executives, a consulting firm that specializes in helping clients achieve breakthrough business results through IT leadership. Manoj brings over thirty years of senior executive leadership skills and technology management experience with domestic and international operations to VIE's clients. Manoj's Information Technology (IT) experience covers a broad array of skills, including Large Scale Technology Infrastructure Management, Outsourcing Management, Information Security Management, Program Management and Enterprise Resource Planning.

Also By Mike Scheuerman and Manoj Garg

The Edge

ISBN: 978-1-483-56064

The Edge is a business novel that educates senior business leaders how to get an edge in running their companies through the strategic use of Information Technology. It gives executives the knowledge and tools to guide their company as it transitions from a mid-level to a high-level competitor in the marketplace. It takes the wondering out of the picture and shows business leaders what software applications and specialized technologies can do. Through its narrative, it simultaneously tells the tale of a company and the struggles of the family that runs it, while describing the best practices of technology management.